LORD JIM

After the Truth

TWAYNE'S MASTERWORK STUDIES

Robert Lecker, General Editor

LORD JIM

After the Truth

Ross C Murfin

Twayne Publishers • New York
Maxwell Macmillan Canada • Toronto
Maxwell Macmillan International • New York Oxford Singapore Sydney

Twayne's Masterwork Studies No. 88

Lord Jim: After the Truth
Ross C Murfin

Twayne Publishers
Macmillan Publishing Company
866 Third Avenue
New York, New York 10022

Maxwell Macmillan Canada, Inc.
1200 Eglinton Avenue East
Suite 200
Don Mills, Ontario M3C 3N1

Macmillan Publishing Company is part of the Maxwell Communication Group of Companies.

Library of Congress Cataloging-in-Publication Data

Murfin, Ross C
Lord Jim : after the truth / Ross C Murfin.
p. cm.—(Twayne's masterwork studies ; no. 88)
Includes bibliographical references and index.
ISBN 0-8057-8094-7 (alk. paper)—ISBN 0-8057-8560-4 (pbk. : alk. paper)
1. Conrad, Joseph, 1857–1924. Lord Jim. I. Title. II. Series.
PR6005.04L743 1992
823′.912—dc20 91-34024
CIP

The paper used in this publication meets the minimum requirements of American National Standard for Information Sciences—Permanence of Paper for Printed Library Materials. ANSI Z3948-1984.

10 9 8 7 6 5 4 3 2 1 (hc)
10 9 8 7 6 5 4 3 2 1 (pb)

Printed in the United States of America

CONTENTS

Joseph Conrad

Portrait by Patrick Donovan, 1989

Note on the References and Acknowledgments

Conrad thought of the 1920 collection of his work as the authoritative edition. This study refers to page numbers in that edition, which was published in the United States by Doubleday and Company and then reprinted—without change in pagination—in subsequent Doubleday editions and, after that, in various Modern Library editions (re)printed by Random House. The Signet (New American) Library edition also follows the 1920 Doubleday text, although page numbers vary.

Chronology: Joseph Conrad's Life and Works

1857	Józef Teodor Konrad Korzeniowski born at Berdyczow (or Berdichev) in the Polish Ukraine, the son of Apollo and Ewa (Bobrowska) Korzeniowski.
1861	Moves to Warsaw, where Apollo, editor of a literary magazine, is arrested and imprisoned by Russian authorities for clandestine political activities.
1862	Forced into exile in Vologda, far northeast of Moscow, when his parents are sentenced to deportation. Develops pneumonia during the journey.
1863	Moves south with his family to Chernikhov. Later visits Uncle Tadeusz Bobrowski with his mother, who is seriously ill.
1865	Death of mother, in April, of tuberculosis. Spends the summer with Uncle Tadeusz. Falls ill on returning home to his father; is taken to Kiev for treatment and back to his uncle's estate for the winter.
1868	Moves to Lvov with his father, who, stricken with tuberculosis, is permitted to return to Poland.
1869	Moves to Cracow with his father, who dies three months later of tuberculosis.
1869–1873	Period of his life about which little is known. Under the care, first, of his father's friend Stefan Buszczynski, he soon after moves to Austrian-occupied Poland with his maternal grandmother, Teofila Bobrowska, ending up, finally, back with his maternal uncle, Tadeusz Bobrowski. As his guardian, Uncle Tadeusz sends Conrad to private tutors and schools in various towns and cities, including Cracow. During this period, Conrad seems to have first envisioned becoming a seaman.
1873	Experiencing chest trouble, goes with his tutor to Switzerland for several months.

1874 Back in Cracow, decides to go to Marseilles, where he has relatives, the Chodzkos. Sails for Martinique as a passenger on the *Mont Blanc.*

1875 Returns to Marseilles and ships out again on the *Mont Blanc,* this time as an apprentice crew member.

1876 Sails again from Marseilles to Martinique on the *Saint-Antoine,* which he serves as a steward and junior officer.

1877 Is perhaps involved in a gunrunning venture aboard the *Tremoline,* which is supplying weapons to Carlists seeking to seize the throne of Spain for Carlos de Bourbon. Squanders a great deal of his uncle's money.

1878 Attempts suicide after allegedly losing at gambling. Sails as an ordinary seaman on the *Mavis,* a British ship, after Uncle Tadeusz arrives to pay off his debts. Visits London and subsequently makes three voyages as a sailor between Lowestoft and Newcastle, during which time he makes progress learning English. Sails for Sydney, Australia, in December.

1879 Spends five months in Australia, returns to London, and sails for Greece on a steamship.

1880 Returns to London, where he studies for the exam to become qualified as a second mate. Passes, and sails for Sydney again, this time as third mate of the *Loch Etive.*

1881 Returns to London and signs on with the *Palestine,* an old coal-carrying vessel headed for Bangkok. Owing to storms, an accident, and subsequent repairs, its departure is delayed almost a year.

1882 The *Palestine* finally sails.

1883 The coal aboard spontaneously combusts. Officers and crew abandon ship and are picked up and taken to Singapore, where they must appear before a court of inquiry. All are found innocent of wrongdoing. (This episode is one of several sources for the *Patna* story in *Lord Jim.*) Returns to London.

1884 Sails to Madras, India, as second mate of the *Riverdale.* On returning to England, first fails but then passes the examination required to become a first mate.

1885 Sails as second mate of the *Tilkhurst,* first to Singapore and then to Calcutta.

1886 Back in England, fails his examination for a master's certificate, becomes a British citizen, and then passes the test for a master's certificate on the second try.

1887 Is injured by a falling spar on a voyage to Java and has to disembark in Singapore, where he remains for 12 months.

Meets Captain Craig of the *Vidar* and eventually sails to Borneo and back four times on that vessel. (These incidents and those of the following year lie behind several novels, including *Lord Jim.*)

1888 Goes to Bangkok to assume command of the *Otago,* which he sails from Singapore to Sidney.

1889 After sailing to Melbourne and South Australia, resigns his command and sails back to England as a passenger on the *Nurnberg.* Begins his first novel, *Almayer's Folly*; then travels to Brussels, where he interviews for the position of captain on a Congo steamboat.

1890 After calling on a sickly cousin, Alexsander Poradowski (and meeting Alexsander's wife, Marguerite, with whom he later develops a close friendship and correspondence), Conrad goes to the Ukraine to see Uncle Tadeusz. Back in Brussels, he learns that, through Marguerite's influence, he has been awarded a three-year appointment in the Congo. What follows becomes the subject matter of "Heart of Darkness": Conrad sails from Bordeaux to the Congo on the *Ville de Maceio* and then serves on the *Roi des Belges,* a Congo River steamship, first as first mate and later as temporary master. Spends four months in the Congo, becomes ill, relinquishes his position, and returns to England.

1891–1892 Visits Marguerite Poradowska in Brussels before recuperating from malaria in London. Sails twice for Australia on the *Torrens,* a clipper ship, as chief officer.

1893 Returns to England, resigns his position on the *Torrens,* and visits Uncle Tadeusz for the last time. Meets his future wife, Jessie George.

1894 Just before visiting Marguerite in Brussels, learns that *Almayer's Folly* has been accepted by Fisher Unwin for publication, on the recommendation of the critic Edward Garnett. Conrad meets Garnett, with whom he is to remain close and establish an important correspondence.

1895 *Almayer's Folly* published. Working on *An Outcast of the Islands,* goes to a spa in Switzerland and courts a French girl but also sees and writes Jessie George frequently.

1896 Proposes to and marries Jessie George. Spends six months in Brittany, where he begins and abandons *The Rescue* and *The Nigger of the "Narcissus." An Outcast of the Islands* published.

1898 Birth of a son, Borys. Spends time with Stephen Crane, begins

	Lord Jim, and, after moving to Kent, begins "Heart of Darkness" as well.
1899	Completes "Heart of Darkness," which comes out in *Blackwood's Magazine,* as does *Lord Jim,* beginning later the same year. Collaborates on *The Inheritors* with Ford Madox Hueffer (later Ford).
1900	*Lord Jim,* now finished, comes out in volume form, as does *The Inheritors.* Begins *Typhoon.*
1901	The Conrads spend two weeks with the Hueffers. Borys becomes seriously ill. Conrad begins *Romance; The Inheritors* published.
1902	Finishes "To-morrow" and *Romance,* begins and ends "The End of the Tether," and publishes *Typhoon* and *Youth* (the volume that includes "Heart of Darkness").
1903	Begins *Nostromo* and publishes *Romance* but calls this a "diastrous year for my work," owing to illness and depression.
1904	Jessie Conrad left lame by a knee injury. Conrad continues work on *Nostromo,* which is being serialized in *T.P.'s Weekly.* The Conrads go to London for treatment of Jessie's knee.
1905	Back to Kent, then on to the Isle of Capri, where Conrad meets Norman Douglas. Back in England, Conrad feels ill. A one-act play, *One Day More,* is performed at the Royal Court Theatre in London.
1906	The Conrads make several trips to Montpellier, France, where Conrad begins *The Secret Agent* and finishes *The Mirror of the Sea,* which is published in December. A second son, John, is born.
1907	While in France, both sons fall ill. The Conrads move to Geneva before returning to England. Conrad begins revising *The Secret Agent* immediately following its serial publication. It appears in September in volume form; in December, Conrad begins what is to become *Under Western Eyes.*
1908	Writes the first installments of *A Personal Record.* Called *Some Reminiscences,* they are published serially in the *English Review.*
1909	Ill much of the year, works on *Under Western Eyes* and begins "The Secret Sharer."
1910	On finishing *Under Western Eyes,* becomes seriously ill. The Conrads move to another house in Kent. Serial publication of *Under Western Eyes* begins.
1911	Although still ill, works on *Chance. Under Western Eyes* pub-

	lished in volume form. Borys Conrad goes to sea on a training ship.
1912	*Some Reminiscences* (later retitled *A Personal Record*) published in volume form. *Chance,* being published serially, makes Conrad a popular success. A short story is begun that is eventually to become *Victory.*
1913	Meets Bertrand Russell. Works on *Victory* and several shorter works. *Chance* published in volume form.
1914	*Victory* completed. The Conrads go to Cracow, Poland, via Hamburg and Berlin, but return to England when World War I breaks out.
1915	Begins *The Shadow-Line. Victory* published, both in serial and in volume form.
1916	Serialization of *The Shadow-Line.* Sails on a vessel whose purpose is to mend torpedo nets.
1917	*The Shadow-Line* published in volume form. Begins what is to become *The Arrow of Gold.* With Jessie, goes to London for medical treatment of her knee.
1918	Completes *The Arrow of Gold,* which begins to appear in serial form. Goes back to work on *The Rescue.*
1919	Finishes *The Rescue,* more than 20 years after beginning it. A theatrical version of *Victory* is produced in London. Begins to adapt *The Secret Agent* for the theater. Accompanies Jessie to Liverpool in December so that she can have knee surgery.
1920	Although ill, Conrad works on *The Rescue,* his dramatic version of *The Secret Agent,* and a play, *Laughing Anne.* Begins researching *Suspense* in the British Museum.
1921	The Conrads travel through France, visit Corsica, and return to London, where Conrad works on *Suspense* and a work that is to become *The Rover.*
1922	Conrad's dramatic version of *The Secret Agent* closes after 10 performances at the Ambassador's Theatre in London.
1923	Goes to Scotland and then to New York from Glasgow on the *Tuscania.* Returns a month later on the *Majestic* and learns that his son Borys has been secretly married for almost a year.
1924	The Conrad's first grandson, Philip, born. Conrad declines a knighthood, suffers a heart attack and dies on 3 August, and is buried in Canterbury on 7 August.
1925	*Suspense* published serially and in volume form.
1926	Publication of *Last Essays.*
1927	An unfinished novel, *The Sisters,* published.

Literary and Historical Context

1

Biographical Background

Joseph Conrad, whose name was originally Józef Teodor Konrad Korzeniowski, was born in 1857 in a part of Poland that, a little less than a century earlier, had been annexed by Russia. Conrad's father, who cared deeply about Polish independence, once said that his son was born not in 1857 but, rather, "in the 85th year of Muscovite oppression."

The nineteenth century was a time in which all Poles felt like people without a country. Russia wasn't the only country that had come to dominate them and attempt to repress their sense of national identity. In 1772 Poland had been carved up and shared by Russia, Prussia, and Austria, only to be redivided in 1793 and again in 1795.

The feeling of being without a country was particularly intense in the Korzeniowski family, for the Korzeniowskis had been landed gentry and, thus, a family with a great deal to lose in the process of national subjugation. That feeling in a sense came to define the very life of young Josef, who was to change countries, languages, and careers, wandering the world to faraway places like the Patusan described in *Lord Jim* (or to the heart of Africa so potently described in *Heart of Darkness*) without ever coming back to claim his place in Poland or his identity as a Pole.

First, though, Josef was to suffer greatly in what had been his family's homeland. Apollo, his father—a poet, playwright, and translator dedicated politically to the cause of Polish independence—was arrested in 1863 for his association with a revolutionary political group. As punishment, Apollo was exiled to the Vologda region of Russia, hundreds of miles north of Moscow. The rest of his family had little choice but to accompany him.

Young Josef nearly died on the trip, and the fierce winter weather soon thereafter affected the health of both his parents. His mother, Ewa, contracted tuberculosis and died in 1865; by 1869 Apollo, too, was dead. Josef, who was now without parents as well as without a country, was adopted by Tadeusz Bobrowski, an uncle on his mother's side of the family.

Uncle Tadeusz tried his best to carry out an unexpected responsibility, sending Josef to Krakow to school and later to Geneva to study with a tutor. His teenage nephew, however, was something of a romantic; he liked neither the tiring challenges of formal education nor the browbeating attempts of the tutor to make him more practical, more worldly. What Josef really wanted to do was join the French merchant navy. In 1874 he finally got his uncle's permission to do just that.

The life that followed must have been more exciting than the life of the student, but it seems to have been no more satisfying. Josef, who sailed to places as far away as Venezuela and the West Indies, lost at love, lost a small fortune gambling, and could have lost his life when he attempted suicide in 1878. It was in 1878, too, that his new identity as a French sailor suffered a serious setback: French immigration authorities prohibited him from continuing to sail on French ships.

Josef had considered switching from the French to the English merchant marine and did so in 1878, thus making a change in direction that turned out to be fortuitous. He was for the next 16 years to sail on British ships, several of which took him to that Eastern world that was to become the setting for *Lord Jim* and a number of other novels. He was eventually to change his name to Joseph Conrad, to become a British citizen in 1887, and to marry a British woman, Jessie George, in 1896. Most important to us, he was at about this same time to exchange the sailor's life for that of the English novelist, publishing novels in what was his third language. In the process of doing all these things he was probably to come as close to adopting a new national identity as the son of an aristocratic Polish patriot could come.

In saying that Conrad came close to becoming English, we must place the accent on the word *close,* for the fact is that Conrad never, in his heart, stopped feeling—or being—Polish. People who met him when he was an old man living in England said he still dressed, looked, and acted like a Polish aristocrat.

Some literary critics, particularly those with a psychoanalytic interest, have treated Conrad's novels as if they were veiled autobiographies. In some of the texts such critics have found what they believe to be evidence that Conrad suffered a lifetime's worth of guilt over the fact that, as a young man, he abandoned Poland and, not too long thereafter, his Polish name. *Lord Jim* is not only one of the novels offered as evidence of this guilt; it is in fact offered as "exhibit A" in the case made by more than one psychoanalytic critic.

Gustav Morf, whose book *The Polish Heritage of Joseph Conrad* receives further attention in the next chapter, first advanced these ideas in 1930. Leo Gurko, one of the critics who in the 1960s was still arguing against Morf's views, nonetheless sums them up most succinctly in his book *Joseph Conrad: Giant in Exile:*

> Jim deserts the *Patna* (Poland) with its cargo of sleeping pilgrims (the Poles faithful to their belief in independence) and jumps into the "everlasting black hole" of the lifeboat (exactly like Conrad's "jump out of his racial associations"). He has been urged to abandon ship by the rascally German captain (Germany was one of Poland's traditional enemies). The *Patna,* however, did not go down; by some miracle she stayed afloat. Some time later she was rescued and towed into port by a French gunboat (France was Poland's traditional friend and ally). Jim tries to exorcise his guilt by standing

> trial and by justifying his actions to Marlow (Conrad addressing himself to his readers, for, according to Morf, his art is an attempt to work out his deeply buried anxieties symbolically, and thus rid himself of them).[1]

Although Gurko finds the argument he summarizes to be as untrue as it is ingenious, he also has to admit that Conrad himself made Morf's reading possible, for the two quotations within the passage quoted above are both by Conrad. The phrase "everlasting black hole," of course, comes from *Lord Jim*. The phrase "jump out of his racial associations" comes from the following passage from Conrad's *A Personal Record,* a passage in which Conrad discusses his decision to go to sea with the French merchant marine: "I verily believe mine was the only case of a boy of my nationality and antecedents taking a, so to speak, standing jump out of his racial surroundings and associations."[2] As Gurko properly suggests, Conrad's reference to his departure from Poland and his family "antecedents" does not entirely justify the view that *Lord Jim* is *about* Conrad's lifelong guilt—just because the novel features a character who takes a jump off a boat! And as other scholars interested not only in *Lord Jim* but also in its possible biographical contexts have suggested, it is not necessary to see the novel as a symbolic representation of its author's psychological reality. Norman Sherry, the critic who has gone the furthest in connecting novel and biography, has suggested that there are far more direct and literal connections to be made between *Lord Jim* and its author's personal experiences.

Sherry begins *Conrad's Eastern World* (1966) by reminding us that Conrad spent 1881 through 1888 sailing those very areas of the globe in which the novel is set, and he establishes the fact that Conrad based characters in other novels (*Almayer's Folly, The Rescue,* and *The Shadow-Line*) on actual people he met while sailing on the *Palestine,* the *Otago,* and the *Vidar.* The sources of the characters and plot incidents to be found in *Lord Jim,* Sherry argues, lie equally or, if anything, even more solidly in Conrad's experiences as a sailor in the Orient.

Conrad's "sources" for *Lord Jim* "were fourfold," Sherry points out; they included "hearsay, observation, personal experience, and reading."[3] As for hearsay, Conrad, like the seamen who make up Marlow's audience, no doubt spent weeks onshore listening to sailors tell stories about people they had met, experiences they had had. As for personal observations and experiences, Conrad himself was subject to a Singapore inquiry into the nature and cause of a disaster at sea. (The *Palestine,* onto which Conrad had shipped as second mate in 1882, had to be abandoned by its officers and crew when the coal it was carrying caught fire.) Finally, where reading is concerned, we can assume that Conrad looked at newspapers during long periods of shore duty—and that he would have been especially interested in stories about ships, sailors, and shipboard scandals.

Of all the stories Conrad ever read about, later heard gossiped about by other sailors, and finally found applicable to his own situation, the story of a ship named the *Jeddah* clearly stands out. Conrad, who himself finally admitted the connection between the historical incident and the novel, would have read about the *Jeddah* scandal in London newspapers in 1880—less than a year before he, as a 24-year-old, embarked on the *Palestine* for the same area of the world in which the *Jeddah* incident had happened.

As for what exactly happened to the *Jeddah,* Sherry sums it up this way in *Conrad's Eastern World:*

> The *Jeddah* was employed in carrying Muslim pilgrims from Singapore to Jeddah. She left Singapore on 17 July 1880 on one of these trips, and after a stormy passage, during which her boilers gave trouble and she began to leak, she was abandoned off Cape Guardafui at 2 A.M. on 8 August 1880 by her captain and her European officers. They were later picked up by the steamship *Scindia* and taken to Aden where they reported that the *Jeddah* was lost with all her passengers. The appearance of the *Jeddah* at Aden a day later with the pilgrims on board, towed in by the S.S. *Antenor,* caused a great scandal both in London and Singapore, and the incident was the subject of an inquiry at Aden, an action for salvage at Singapore, a debate in the Singapore Legislative Assembly, and a question in the House of Commons. (Sherry 1966, 43)

The main parallels to the story Conrad tells in *Lord Jim* are too painfully obvious to need pointing out. Suffice it to say about the minor ones that although Conrad changes *Jeddah* to *Patna* and, less significantly, *Antenor* to *Avondale,* he doesn't even bother to change the name of the place—Aden—to which his "fictional" ship is towed.

And yet, as Sherry and any number of other scholars who have written on biographical sources would remind us, Conrad *was* a writer of fiction, and *Lord Jim* is *not* just an account of the *Jeddah* incident with (a few of the) names changed to protect the guilty. Conrad himself issued that same reminder to one A. T. Saunders, a clerk working for an Australian shipping firm who first inquired into the parallels between Conrad's novels and actual incidents that took place in the Far East. In a letter that begins by implying Saunders has indeed discovered some of the sources of his inspiration ("You are a terror for tracking people out!"), Conrad goes on to remind his enthusiastic correspondent of the limits of that discovery. "After all," the author points out, gently but sternly to the scholar-detective, "I *am* a writer of fiction; and it is not what actually happened, but the manner of presenting it that settles the literary and even the moral value of my work" (quoted in Sherry 1966, 295).

The most basic pieces of evidence that *Lord Jim* is fiction and not historical fact are the differences—some tiny, some profound—between it and the *Jeddah* story. The *Jeddah* carried 953 pilgrims and lifeboats for roughly a third of that number; the *Patna* carried 800 people and 7 lifeboats. The *Jeddah,* which was imperiled by a storm, leaked for several days before its officers gave up on the ship; the *Patna* crisis, which was brought about by a floating wreck and not a storm, happened extremely suddenly.

More important, as Sherry points out, "There were certain circumstances in the case of the *Jeddah* which might be thought to have lessened the offence of the captain and the officers in deserting her" (Sherry 1966, 52). For one thing, the wife of the captain was on board, and even the assessor at the inquiry later expressed his belief that, had she not been, the captain would not have abandoned ship. For another, whereas most of the *Patna* pilgrims sleep while the ship's cowardly crew jumps, the officers of the *Jeddah* jumped, in part, because the pilgrims had armed themselves with knives and clubs and, after threatening the master and his wife, had actually attacked the crew. Indeed, A. P. Williams, first mate of the *Jeddah,* had not wanted to leave the ship but had been thrown overboard by the pilgrims and picked up by the captain.

Notwithstanding several significant differences between the plot of *Lord Jim* and the story of the *Jeddah* incident, the parallels are many and striking, and although the novel is a work of art, not a chronicle, we can better appreciate it *as* art by knowing how it is (and, therefore, how it is not) grounded in historical incident. The *Jeddah,* like the *Patna,* carried far fewer lifeboats than were needed to accommodate passengers and crew: this inadequate situation strongly influenced what happened, both on the real craft and on the fictional one crafted by Joseph Conrad.

There is an undeniable parallel to be found between Conrad's marvelous character of the French lieutenant and a real person involved in the *Jeddah* affair, a Mr. Campbell, first mate of the *Antenor.* According to the "Report on the Action for Salvage Brought against the *Jeddah*" published in the *Straits Times Overland Journal,* "taking the *Jeddah* in tow was accomplished after considerable difficulty, and with the exercise of much patience, skill, and ingenuity, the Chief Officer [of the *Antenor*] steered the *Jeddah* himself."[4] (In *Conrad's Eastern World* Sherry writes: "Conrad must have known of Mr. Campbell's actions, for the lieutenant of the French gunboat which towed in the *Patna* acts in a remarkably similar way, although he is heavily disguised as a Frenchman"; Sherry 1966, 55.) And there are still other characters in *Lord Jim* who are similarly close to—and changed from—historical originals. Engineer George, who dies on deck just before Jim abandons ship (and whose place in the lifeboat Jim takes), may have been suggested by the second mate of the *Jeddah,* who also died in the act of desertion—not of a heart attack but, rather, when one of the lifeboats sank.

But of all the people involved in the *Jeddah* affair who seem more or less like characters in *Lord Jim,* A[ugustine]. P[odmore]. Williams, the ship's first mate, is most worthy of our attention. Sherry calls him nothing less than "Conrad's inspiration for the whole first part of the novel: Williams, like Jim, was from a parsonage, he was the last officer to leave the *Jeddah,* he figured prominently in the subsequent Inquiry, and he afterwards, like Jim, became a ship-chandler's water-clerk in Singapore. Unlike Jim, he worked out his salvation this way, growing fat and prospering" (Sherry 1966, 66). There are, to be sure, a few differences between Conrad's character and the *Jeddah's* first mate. (Of these, the most important are that Williams, not wanting to jump, was thrown overboard; in addition, his certificate was not suspended as a result of the inquiry.) But the similarities are greater in number. Like Jim, Williams was trained as a sailor on a training ship; his appearance, which we know about through photographs, matches Conrad's descriptions of Jim's almost perfectly; after the *Jeddah* incident, Williams tried to live down his past, first as a sailor (he probably even sailed with Conrad on the *Vidar* in 1882) and later as a water clerk to a ship's chandler. He settled, finally, near the Berau River in Borneo and married a Eurasian woman, much as Jim married Jewel. So close is the resemblance between Williams and Jim that Williams's own daughter, having read the novel, remarked that Conrad's protagonist must have been based on her father.

If Conrad didn't sail with Williams on the *Vidar* a couple of years after the *Jeddah* incident, he probably did get to know Williams on or around the Berau River in Borneo, to which Conrad's ships sailed carrying goods to traders. (Patusan is clearly modeled after this area of what was then Dutch East Borneo.) Certainly, we know that Conrad *did* get to know Jim Lingard, who had been brought from Europe to reinvigorate the trading business of his uncle William Lingard (a man who must have served as partial inspiration for the character of Stein). A. P. Williams knew both of the Lingard men; in fact, his children played with Jim Lingard's children. Thus, Conrad could easily have come to know Williams through his acquaintance with Jim Lingard.

The interesting thing is that Williams doesn't seem to have served as model for the Jim we meet in the second half of Conrad's novel.

Whereas Williams's career almost exactly parallels Jim's up to the point where he goes to work for a ship's chandler, Jim Lingard's career seems to have served as the inspiration for Lord Jim's Patusan career. Sherry has noted, "There is a change in the character of the hero in *Lord Jim* once he goes to Patusan" (Sherry 1966, 135). That change, I would argue, occurs because Conrad's model for Jim has shifted—from A. P. Williams to Jim Lingard.

The shift was no doubt made possible or even easy by the fact that Williams and Lingard in some ways resembled one another. (For one thing, Lingard, like Williams, lived with a native woman who may, together with Williams's wife, have been the partial inspiration for Jewel.) There were other ways, though, in which they were quite unalike. Although Williams became fairly prosperous, he never became what Jim Lingard did, namely, a kind of English rajah. A man with a servant (named Lias, the servant may have suggested to Conrad the character of Tamb' Itam), Lingard enjoyed from the people of Dutch East Borneo something that was little less than worship. If he was never called "Tuan," he certainly might have been.

It is in some ways even easier to believe that Jim Lingard served as the model for the Jim we meet in the second half of the book than it is to believe that A. P. Williams served as the model for the Jim we meet in the first half. Not only do we know that Conrad met Lingard; we also know that Lingard served as the model for Captain Tom Lingard, a character who figures strongly in several other Conrad novels. Conrad's fascination with Lingard, however, is not so interesting or admirable as his interest in Williams; Lingard was a fairly typical "Great White Master" type, the product of an imperialism and colonialism that Conrad approved of but we do not. If the character of Jim becomes less interesting, less real-seeming, and less attractive once Jim settles on Patusan and becomes lord to a respectful, darker-skinned people, it may well be because political consciousness—as well as Conrad's model—has undergone a change. We need not disapprove of Conrad's admiration of a man like Lingard or even of the later character of Lord Jim. We do, however, need to see it as a historically determined attitude, even as our changed attitude has been historically determined by a century of struggles for independence from imperial and colonial rule and rulers.

Jim is not the only character in *Lord Jim* who seems to have been inspired by several historical personages. The character of Jewel has already been mentioned; as for the trader Stein, he bears a resemblance not only to Jim Lingard's uncle, William Lingard, but also to A. R. Wallace, a naturalist and bird collector whose book *Malay Archipelago* profoundly influenced Conrad. (Conrad's depictions of the rajahs, of warring factions on Patusan, and even of Doramin and his wife owe a great deal to Wallace.) Moreover, we oversimplify things greatly if we say that Stein was inspired by just two people: Lingard and Wallace. Wallace's young assistant, Charles Allen, is in some ways more like Stein than Wallace is. (Remember that Stein started out as assistant to a great naturalist.) And there was, in addition, a great German naturalist in the area collecting for the Leyden Museum. His name? Dr. Bern*stein*.

Given that Stein is a composite of three or four historical figures (plus of a tremendous amount of purely imaginative input), it is hardly surprising to learn that Conrad's understanding of the Malay archipelago is the product of three or four books on the area besides Wallace's. (In addition, of course, it is the product of a considerable amount of personal experience in the area.) Major F. McNair's *Perak and the Malays* includes the names Doramin, Tamb' Itam, and Tunku Allang, as well as the story of a night attack like Jim's on Sherif Ali's camp. From books by Sir Edward Belcher and F. S. Marryat, Conrad may have come up with the idea of Gentleman Brown: they mention a character named Brownrigg who did much of what Conrad's nemesis ultimately does.

Whereas Wallace is but one of three or four authors whose accounts of Malaysia influenced Conrad and but one of three or four historical prototypes for the character of Stein, he was also the prototype for several characters, insofar as he was once caught and confined by a rajah just as Jim is caught and confined by Rajah Allang (whose name came not from Wallace's book but, rather, from

McNair's). Moreover, if we think back on all the information set forth above, we can see that he is hardly the only "real-life" character who, on one hand, is but one model for a fictional character and, on the other hand, a model for several characters. For example, insofar as William Lingard is a trader who turns over business that once was his to a young protégé, he is like Stein. However, to the extent that he is an older man whose failing business is taken over by a young man fresh from England, he is not unlike Cornelius—a very different character indeed from Stein.

These almost-endless complications are not important to remember, but it *is* important to realize their existence. They return us, after all, to the two most significant questions that have been raised, implicitly if not explicitly, throughout this chapter on the biographical background of *Lord Jim*.

One of those questions concerns how the novel can *be* a novel and yet be so clearly grounded in real people and real events. A realization that the fictional Jim can be the real Wallace, Williams, and Lingard—even while the real Lingard's real uncle can have become part of several (different and opposed) characters—helps us to get a better sense of just how far from, as well as how close to, historical reality Conrad's fiction is. The best analogy might be that of the relationship between dreams and actual experience. Just as one real person may become the inspiration for several dream figures (psychoanalysts following Freud would refer to this as "dream multiplication"), so one dream figure may, on reflection, remind us of several real people we know. (When this happens, "dream compression" has occurred.)

Are dreams *like* reality? Do they represent it? Without reality, certainly, they could hardly be "made up." And yet we all know that dreams are profoundly different from life—with the accent on *profoundly*. They are as different from personal history as *Lord Jim* is from history and biography. Like *Lord Jim*, they are instead an imaginative re-presentation of life, a way by which, through analysis, we may come to understand it—its hidden motivations and its sometimes-subsurface web of connections.

The other, seminal question we ought to reconsider in light of the almost-endless complications regarding "who became whom" is whether *Lord Jim* can be read psychologically. Was Gustav Morf justified in seeing, as the background to *Lord Jim,* not Conrad's experiences as a sailor in and around places like Singapore, Aden, and Borneo but, rather, his decision to "jump" what seemed a sinking Polish "ship" and into the "lifeboat" of the French merchant marine?

What complicated associations like those between Stein and Lingard and Wallace and Allen and Berstein should tell us is that Morf *may* be justified in suggesting that Conrad's decision to leave Poland behind is one biographical context of *Lord Jim.* After all, dozens of such contexts have been suggested, not just by Morf and Sherry but by other critics as well. (John Batchelor, in a book on *Lord Jim* published in 1988, argues rather convincingly that Jim is a composite of one James Brooke, a white man who helped rule Sarawak, Borneo, and the American novelist Stephen Crane, "the blue-eyed son of a Methodist pastor" who was as different in age from Conrad as Jim is different from Marlow and whose death "was intimately bound up with the writing of the novel."[5] If Jim can be a little bit derived from people so different as Stephen Crane, James Brooke, A. P. Williams, Jim Lingard, and even, to a lesser extent, A. R. Wallace, he can surely have lying, somewhere in his makeup as a character, the partial identity of his author, Joseph Conrad.

What is important to realize in considering questions about which sources are credible is that Jim is neither Conrad nor A. P. Williams, just as the *Patna* is neither Poland nor the *Jeddah.* (Neither is it the *Palestine,* the ship that caught fire and caused Conrad to be subject to an inquiry; nor is it the real ship named the *Patna* that "frequented Singapore during the 1880s" and that Batchelor believes "must have been Conrad's immediate source; Batchelor, 59.) Rather, what we can say—in addition to saying that Jim and the ship he jumps from are the product of all of these and many, many more influences as well—is that Conrad may have become interested in the *Jeddah* story, consciously or subconsciously, because he had himself once abandoned ships in trouble. He had left the *Palestine* on fire much as the officers of the *Jeddah* had left their ship foundering in a storm. He had, moreover, in a different place and way, left old and powerful Polish associations behind and taken a long and no-doubt-difficult leap into an uncertain new life.

2

The Importance of the Work

The publication date of *Lord Jim* (1900), though in some ways a mere accident of history and of calendar construction, is in other ways suggestive of the significance of Conrad's novel, for although *Lord Jim* is an intricate and important work in its own right, it also stands at a critical juncture between past and present, between historical and aesthetic eras we tend to call Victorian on one hand and modern on the other. As such, it serves as a kind of last repository for nineteenth-century attitudes and literary conventions while, more important, foreshadowing the themes and methods of twentieth-century works.

It is common for people to debate, during the last decade of a century, whether the year that ends in two or more zeros (1700, 1800, 1900, 2000) belongs to the century that is ending or to the new one just beginning. Some would say that if the year 1 was the century's first year, then the year numbered 100 would be the hundredth and therefore last year of the century. Those on the other side of this admittedly trivial debate tend to argue that we have to think of the first year A.D. as the year 0, not the year 1, and that, anyway, the year 2000 will psychologically and symbolically mark the beginning of the new century. Certainly, the past is on their side. Newspaper accounts of the beginning of our own, twentieth century suggest that, in the minds of most people, it began on 1 January 1900. It takes little imagination to guess that the wildest New Year's Eve parties that lie in our own future will begin on 31 December 1999, and not on 31 December 2000.

The point of this seeming digression is that *Lord Jim* is much like the year in which it was published—that is, we can look at it, as some critics have, as the last novel of the nineteenth century, or, as others have, as the first novel of the twentieth. Looked at as the last nineteenth-century novel, *Lord Jim* is a romantic poem in prose, a belated adventure tale, and/or a realistic depiction of the East by a man who had been there and come back to represent in fiction the reality he had experienced. Looked at as a twentieth-century novel, *Lord Jim* is a profound work of psychological realism that can profitably be seen in light of modern psychoanalytic theory, a symbol-laden text that skips back and forth across time and adumbrates the stream-of-consciousness style of Virginia Woolf and James Joyce, and/or a puzzlelike narrative structure that looks forward to works as recent as *V* and *Gravity's Rainbow*, by Thomas Pynchon.

Looked at as a last romantic poem, *Lord Jim* is, as David Thorburn has suggested, a kind of rewritten version of Coleridge's *Rime of the Ancient Mariner,* a work in which a man passes on his tale of crime, guilt, punishment, and atonement to another man, a wedding guest he just happens to meet. (Jim recounts his story to Marlow, who later relates it to an audience that, in a profound sense, includes us.) Conrad's novel is also like a poem by Wordsworth, in which moral truths emerge, if and when they emerge, from the recollection of the past in the present.

Looked at as an adventure tale, *Lord Jim* is a somewhat typical nineteenth-century romance about a young man's seafaring career, beset with danger and marked by critical mistakes, in which a love interest develops in a faraway, romantic setting. It is a tale that comes to a chilling and bloody end, thanks to the treacherous interference of a classic villain figure, the awful and ruthless buccaneer, "Gentleman" Brown. As the next chapter will show, several of the early reviewers saw the novel this way, expressing gratitude that Conrad had chosen not to write the kind of realistic or naturalistic account of the bleak urban scene that had become common by the end of the nineteenth century. (As the next chapter will also show, there have been twentieth-century critics, from F. R. Leavis to the contemporary Marxist Fredric Jameson, who have condemned the novel to the extent that it is a conventional nineteenth-century adventure-romance.)

Looked at as neither a romantic poem nor an adventure tale but, rather, a novel at once realistic and grounded in history, *Lord Jim* is a work that supplies us with notably accurate observations of the East—its natives, its immigrants, its colonial traders and rulers—even as it chronicles, in thin disguise, historical events and personages that dominated the newspapers during the period in which Conrad sailed the seas around Malaysia.

As the previous chapter establishes—with a degree of detail that need not be repeated here—*Lord Jim* has been said to be based on an infamous scandal involving the *Jeddah,* a ship carrying pilgrims that ran into trouble in a storm and was consequently abandoned by its European officers and crew. Conrad, who would have read about the incident in London newspapers, may have met—and may even have sailed with—the first mate of the *Jeddah,* A. P. Williams. Norman Sherry, the scholar best known for establishing historical parallels in Conrad's work, has suggested that the character of Jim is a realistic composite of Williams and one Jim Lingard, an Englishman who controlled much of the trade in the Berau River area of Dutch East Borneo.

The view of *Lord Jim* as a romantic adventure tale on one hand and as a realistic-historical novel on the other seems almost contradictory, and yet nineteenth-century fiction had been ushered in by the Waverley novels of Sir Walter Scott, novels that had effectively combined romance and reality, history and adventure. Nineteenth-century fiction, moreover, had begun to come to closure with the works of Robert Louis Stevenson, a novelist who, like Conrad, had combined history, adventure, and romance in tales of good boys and bad buccaneers. There is a way in which *Lord Jim* can profitably be seen as the end of something Sir Walter Scott had begun.

But just as the year 1900, although it may technically be the end of the nineteenth century, is more generally and more credibly viewed as the beginning of our own twentieth century, so *Lord Jim,* although it is grounded undeniably in history and although it describes reality through conventions of fiction passed down by a century's worth of literary giants, is nonetheless more generally and usefully viewed as the beginning of modern British fiction. Certainly, the novel appears at the beginning of far more university courses in the modern or twentieth-century British novel than it does at the end of similar, chronologically organized courses in Victorian or nineteenth-century British fiction.

The reasons, though many and complicated, can be summarized as follows. *Lord Jim,* like twentieth-century novels in English, is more interested in depicting the complexity of human psychology realistically than it is in reproducing a shared external environment. Like authors to come after him, Conrad relies heavily on symbols: not symbols that, one by one, correspond to fairly obvious ideas or ideals ("Old Glory" symbolizes the United States) but, rather, a complex network of symbols that, though ambiguous in and by themselves, work together to suggest meaning. Finally, *Lord Jim* is a complex narrative experiment: a tale of a tale of a tale that implicates the reader in novel ways and that seems, finally, to have its own kind of symbolic power.

Sigmund Freud, the great Austrian physician who is generally agreed to be the founder of modern psychoanalytic theory, created a model for understanding human psychology according to which human beings have unconscious as well as conscious wishes. Freud stated that there are (a) motivations for behavior and even aspects of our identity that we know about and (b) other motivations and/or selves whose very existence we are largely unconscious of. Sometimes these buried, or repressed, wishes, fears, and aspects of the self surface in dreams, but dreams themselves, in Freud's view, involve a form of censorship. Full of symbols that disguise as much as they reveal, they yield their true subject matter only when subjected to careful, even painstaking professional analysis.

In *Lord Jim,* published the same year Freud published his famous *Interpretation of Dreams,* Conrad presents us with a character who implies a quite-similar interest in and view of human psychology. Jim consciously conceives of himself as a hero. This self-conception corresponds with publicly acceptable standards—with exemplary views of human identity taught by parsons and professors and available in literature from the epic to the adventure tale. At key moments in his life, however, Jim seems to act as if he is some *other* person—a person whose behavior utterly surprises him, one whose motivations he does not know.

One of those moments, of course, is the appropriately dark and confusing one in which Jim, almost unconsciously, jumps from the *Patna.* Not only does Jim not know why he jumped; a short while later, he cannot even fully believe that he *has* jumped: "I had jumped . . . it seems" is what he later tells Marlow. Jim spends a lifetime trying to prove that the man who seems to have jumped was not himself (as he would seem to have been), only to have that other self surface once more toward the end of his life—and story.

Marlow seems fascinated by Jim because Jim's doubleness seems to teach some kind of truth about all human beings. What, after all, caused rock-solid Captain Brierly to jump suicidally from his ship if not some second, repressed self—a self that the public "inquiry" into Jim's behavior has made him face up to? Understanding Jim's story is like understanding a dream; Jim is enigmatic, not fully knowable. But that understanding, Marlow seems to feel, would help him and his audience (including us) to penetrate an important darkness.

Conrad renders the complexity of psychology realistically not through the kind of details common to realistic novels—for the mind is not like a London slum or, at least, not *literally* like one—but, rather, through a complex set of symbols, each of which is dependent on others to suggest meaning. The huge flake of rust Jim sees below decks on the *Patna,* the fragile plate that seems ready to give way to the water's onrush, might not itself seem or be able to signify the fragility of Jim's conscious self-conception, of the identity he has maintained while holding back dark and powerful forces. But in combination with, say, the floating derelict, it manages to acquire just that kind of signifying power, for the derelict (the very word is suggestive) is a second image that makes us think about the fact that our security is terribly fragile and capable of being suddenly ruptured by things invisible, lying just under the surface.

Conrad's symbols are somewhat different from those found in nineteenth-century texts (the river as life in *Huckleberry Finn*), insofar as they not only need one another to work but cannot so easily be pinned down or explained. As soon as we say that the rusty plate is Jim's fragile, conscious self, we are left to deal with the fact that the plate doesn't flake off and let in the flood, whereas Jim's idealized self-conception does. As soon as we define the derelict as the dark, unknown self just waiting to check our progress in some black moment, we may want to define it differently: as that unforeseen event which will *allow* our insidious, impulsive, or instinctual self to emerge. Just as two symbols can suggest the same thing, so one symbol can suggest different—even opposite—things. The symbolism of *Lord Jim* is like the symbolism of dreams. More to the point, it is like the symbolism of poetry from T. S. Eliot's *The Waste Land* to John Ashberry's *A Double Dream of Spring*.

The complexity of the symbolism of *Lord Jim* is matched only by that of a narrative structure that looks forward to James Joyce's *Ulysses* or Thomas Pynchon's *V.* The novel begins with an apparently omniscient narrator introducing us to a character who "got his living as a ship-chandler's water-clerk" in various Eastern ports. Within a couple of pages, however, we have dropped back in time to the point that Jim is a boy in a parsonage. Then he is on a training ship; then, suddenly, he is on the *Patna* and something—we are not sure what—has happened. The fourth chapter begins with an account of the official inquiry into what happened; in the fifth the narrative is turned over to a character, Marlow, who has attended the inquiry and become interested in Jim's story.

By the time we reach the seventh chapter of the novel, Jim is narrating *to* Marlow events that happened between the time of the *Patna*'s collision and that of the inquiry. Later, we join Marlow's audience of men seated in the darkness, hearing of what happened to Jim after the inquiry. Ultimately, the book has us reading Marlow's written account of what happened to Jim just before he died—an account sent in a package to a "privileged man" who at one point had helped make up Marlow's seated audience.

The incredible—and incredibly modern—complexity of the novel's narrative structure has a complex effect on the reader. The "distortions" of chronology force us to consider possible, significant likenesses between events that happened at different times; we are made to look for underlying rather than arbitrary or superficial connections, much as we are made to look, given the book's psychological focus, for the underlying causes of behavior. That the tale is really more of a "tale of a tale of a tale" gives this already-complicated narrative a kind of symbolic power and value not entirely unlike that of the rusty plate or floating derelict.

Read symbolically, the concentric circles of the novel's narrative structure would seem to suggest two things: (a) that the search for "truth" inevitably involves us in a multilayered search for truth in and through others and (b) that these digressive searches, even as they seem to carry us away from our object, paradoxically carry us toward it. We may know Jim better than Marlow does *because* we know him through Marlow; Marlow may know Jim better than Jim knows himself *because* his experience is at one remove from Jim's.

This brings us, finally, to the way in which *Lord Jim* is most decidedly modern: it is a novel that implicates the reader. Hearing Jim tell Marlow what happened in the lifeboat makes us feel a certain kinship with Marlow, for we, too, are listeners. Later, we feel that same kinship with Marlow's audience as Marlow, the tale-teller, suddenly becomes like Conrad. Authors and audiences, narrators and narratees—all become interidentified in a way that makes the search for truth about human identity seem a collective enterprise.

In writing about *Lord Jim* and, by a typically Conradian extension, about the Lord Jim within *Lord Jim*, we are implicated in that enterprise. Whether we write a study such as this one or a course paper that has caused us to consult books such as this one, we become, as we write, but the latest of those "privileged" people who have discussed the "story of the story of the story of" a complex, multifaceted identity, the truth about which may just be the truth about all of us.

3

Critical Reception

Lord Jim was generally well received when published in 1900. Reviewers liked the novel's romance, the faraway feelings it evoked, and the original poetry of Conrad's language, which they found analogously beautiful to the Pacific islands and inhabitants depicted in the text. The character of Jewel was appreciated, as was her relationship with Jim and the sad but powerful conversation Marlow has with Jewel—in Jim's absence. Reviewers were also fascinated by Stein, whom one reviewer referred to as "a wonderful creation," a "figure that fills the eye."[1] What the early critics decidedly did not like, however, was Conrad's way of telling his story, the odd narrative method that gives structure to the novel.

In an unsigned review in the Manchester *Guardian,* the novel was called "a memorable event," a work of "remarkable originality." Admitting that the character of Jewel might be a touch too conventional, the reviewer nonetheless went on to lavish praise, saying that "she may be a convention, but, if so, [she is] one we cannot spare," given "the purity of her emotions, her natural nobility, her impregnable simplicity" (Sherry 1973, 111–13).

The reviewer was far less impressed with the "mechanism" of the story. Finding it "curious at best," he says that any "night" on which

Marlow managed to tell the tale must have been "artificially prolonged." He finds bothersome, in general, Conrad's decision to present not a tale but a tale of a man telling a tale, and he describes as "distracting" the fact that the whole last movement of the story has supposedly been mailed to "a privileged [former] auditor"—a man who has consequently and mysteriously made the contents of that package available to us (Sherry 1973, 111–12).

The reviewer for the *Academy*—who may have been Edward Garnett—praises the novel's detail, its resulting mood, and the effect of both on the reader: "all [is] done with a poetical, romantic, half-wistful air for which we go in vain to any other English writer" (Sherry 1973, 115). But like the *Guardian* reviewer, the reviewer for the *Academy* singles out as a major sticking point the novel's claim that Marlow can tell Jim's story in an evening: "This after-dinner story, told without a break, consists of about 99,000 words. Now it is unreasonable to suppose that the narrator spoke at a rate greater than 150 words a minute, which means that he was telling that after-dinner story to his companions for eleven solid hours" (Sherry 1973, 117).

The *Academy* reviewer, like the *Guardian* reviewer, generally disapproves of the novel's narrative method. Attributing to the Russian novelist Ivan Turgenev the "convention" of an omniscient narrator "hand[ing] over" the story to a character in the story, "a storyteller in an arm chair," he goes on to call Conrad's use of the convention "mechanical and not credible" (Sherry 1973, 116). And he especially dislikes the achronological nature of Conrad's narrative-within-a-narrative. Why do we first meet Jim as a water clerk? he wonders. "Why not have begun with . . . the words, 'Originally, he came from a parsonage'?" (Sherry 1973, 116).

Again and again, the reviews said the same things when they were praising or condemning *Lord Jim*. The *Spectator* liked it for being "detached from 'actuality,'" for keeping "aloof from great cities" and showing the "natives" of the Malay archipelago," together with the "strange glamour of their landscape" (Sherry 1973, 119). The *Pall Mall Review* complained about "a very broken-backed narrative," a "formless novel" in which everything that is described as happening after the *Patna* incident "seems to be an afterthought" (Sherry 1973, 123). The London *Daily News* called the book "grandiose" and "poetic" but complained that, in terms of its chronology and structure, the story "wanders back and forth," creating "obstructions set in the way of the reader" (Sherry 1973, 124).

Only one reviewer, the anonymous critic writing in the *Speaker*, got considerably beyond the usual statements of praise and censure. That critic, after saying some fairly typical things about "Mr. Conrad's command of the language" and describing as the novel's "most beautiful passage" the one depicting "Marlow's interchange with Jewel," goes on to praise Conrad not for writing poetically about the Malay archipelago and people but, rather, for having addressed "a problem of universal interest" through what the critic calls a "psychological" novel (Sherry 1973, 123, 120).

As for the narrative "arrangement," the *Speaker* reviewer calls it "original and effective," reserving praise, in particular, for the achronological ordering of events, which are said to be "forestalled" so that "the reader" will not be "distracted by the movement of plot or story from seeing their meaning." Noting how "the story doubles back in itself continuously when a theory of conduct wants illustrating," the reviewer congratulates Conrad for having "solved one of the great difficulties of the philosophical romance" (Sherry 1973, 122).

It is the terms of this review that find their way into later critical assessments of the novel. As different as readings of *Lord Jim* are from decade to decade, critics have by and large agreed that the novel is philosophical, psychological, and, structurally speaking, a complex but effective narrative. And they have been considerably less interested—until very recently, anyway—in the poetic rendering of the East, the romantic depiction of its people.

Gustav Morf, in an early study entitled *The Polish Heritage of Joseph Conrad* (1930), developed the idea that *Lord Jim* is a psychological novel, arguing that it is an "autobiographical" and "symbolical" work, the "confession" of a "man tortured by doubts and nightmarish fears."[2] Basing his critical "analysis" on the theories of "Freud and

Jung" (Morf, 149), Morf proceeds by arguing that *Lord Jim* "is built up of the same elements as a dream" and that, consequently, it can be analyzed much in the same way that dreams are analyzed (Morf, 153).

Morf begins by focusing on Jim's interchange with Gentleman Brown, showing how characters in Conrad can represent the alter egos, the higher or lower selves, of other characters. Then, in a parallel way, he explores the relationship between Jim and Conrad, arguing that the hero of *Lord Jim,* who is physically Conrad's opposite, is the author's alter ego, or dream counterpart, a kind of disguised self-projection. Conrad's "readings," like Jim's, "and not the sight of the sea . . . awoke in him the desire to become a sailor" (Morf, 162). Before he took up the French and later the English seafaring life, Conrad—whose last name was then Korzeniowski—was referred to by Polish peasants and servants as Pan Josef, which means something like "Lord Joseph." Conrad, like Jim, eventually stopped using his family name.

What does Morf make of these parallels? He sees the tale as being analogous to a dream projection of Conrad's guilt for having abandoned Poland in his youth—for having jumped his national ship during a trying and threatening time. *Lord Jim,* Morf postulates, is the nightmarish "expression of Conrad's fear that the desertion of his native country might ultimately prove a fault by which he had forfeited his honor" (Morf, 164). It is a view of *Lord Jim*—and Conrad—that has been debated ever since the publication of Morf's book. Leo Gurko has since argued, in *Joseph Conrad: Giant in Exile* (1962), that Morf's theory may not be "true" and that, in any case, "to read *Lord Jim* as a compendium of clues to Conrad's personal feelings is to shrink its range of discourse" (Gurko, 16, 18). In *Joseph Conrad: A Psychoanalytic Biography,* Bernard C. Meyer has termed Morf's theory "plausible," quoting Conrad's comment in *A Personal Record* that "I verily believe mine was the only case of a boy of my nationality and antecedents taking a, so to speak, standing jump out of his racial surroundings and associations."[3]

In the decade following the publication of Morf's still-debated study, F. R. Leavis published *The Great Tradition,* a book on George

Eliot, Henry James, and Joseph Conrad that, like Morf's book on Conrad's Polish heritage, still manages to stir lively debate. Leavis didn't advance the view of *Lord Jim* as a psychological (or philosophical) novel; instead, he contested the early reviewers' notion that the novel is to be valued for its highly poetical language and for its representation, through that language, of a romantic, faraway, South Pacific realm. In one of the most famous attacks on Conrad ever published, Leavis condemned Conrad for his "adjectival insistence upon inexpressible and incomprehensible mystery," on his tendency "not to magnify but rather to muffle" with words.[4]

Although those harsh comments were directed specifically at *Heart of Darkness*, Leavis went on to dismiss fully half of *Lord Jim* as yet another of Conrad's "adjectival studies," this one "in the Malayan exotic." He called the Patusan portions of the novel "wearying" by virtue of their "eloquence," "exoticism," and "'picturesque' human interest." What he praised was "the first part of the book, the account of the inquiry and the desertion of the *Patna*, the talk with the French lieutenant." The "romance that follows," in addition to being marred by "linguistic excesses," has no "inevitability" as "a continued exhibition of Jim's case" (Leavis, 190).

Dorothy Van Ghent, writing five years after Leavis, advances the claim made by the reviewer writing in the *Speaker* and developed by Morf, namely, that *Lord Jim* is a great psychological novel. In *The English Novel: Form and Function* (1953), she picks up specifically on the notion that Conrad's characters are often doubled and develops Morf's reading of the relationship between Jim and Gentleman Brown. Morf had argued that Jim cannot condemn Brown because Brown represents the "*evil . . . within himself*" (Morf, 158); Van Ghent calls Jim's compact with Brown "a compact with his own unacknowledged guilt," though it is also, she argues, "at the same time, and paradoxically, a lonely act of faith with the white men 'out there.'"[5]

Van Ghent goes on to treat Jim's jump as "a paradigm of the encounters of the conscious personality with the stranger within." Noting that the encounter "is a frightful one," Van Ghent suggests that Jim's response to it is to try to "exorcise the stranger, in a fierce, long, concentrated effort to be his opposite." The irony is that Jim, like Sophocles's Oedipus, in trying to flee "in the opposite direction" of what he fears is his dark "destiny," runs "straight into it" (Van Ghent, 229). In that sense he repeats what happens to one of his other psychological doubles, Captain Brierly. Brierly, in trying to avoid the possibility of becoming a Jim, becomes by his suicide exactly "what he was trying to avoid" (Van Ghent, 241).

Thomas Moser, writing in the mid-1960s, continued to develop, if not Morf's idea that *Lord Jim* offers a revealing study of Conrad's psychology, at least Van Ghent's notion that the novel provides a fascinating psychological study of its main character, Jim. Standing back not just from the novel but from Conrad's entire canon, Moser divides Conrad's characters into three major types: (a) the simple hero (such as the French lieutenant), (b) the vulnerable hero (the subject of psychological studies, the "complicated character," the "man with the 'plague spot'"), and (c) the perceptive hero (the man who analyzes himself, in part by studying other characters).[6] Marlow, for Moser, is the perceptive hero of *Lord Jim*.

Moser's study is interesting because of the way in which it focuses on Marlow as a complex character, rather than as merely the unconvincing vehicle of a "broken-backed" narrative. Moser also relates Marlow's role as a perceiver to that of the reader—who must perceive Jim through Marlow's perceptions. Marlow, Moser says, "gives the reader a sense of actuality"; he is, for the reader, "Jim's interpreter." At the same time, Moser points out, Marlow provides the text with a certain degree of uncertainty. Stein's famous narrative on "how to be" is "qualified by the consciousness of primary narrator, Marlow," and since "Marlow is not at all sure about Stein's advice," *we* may wonder how fairly it has been represented (Moser, 39–40).

Moser's views are also important in that he reasserts the idea, first published in the *Speaker* and later refined by Joseph Warren Beach, that the achronology of the narrative is beneficial and even artful. When the reader reads first about Brierly's jump and then later about Jim's earlier one, the result is an understanding: that "Jim's jump to save his skin is as reprehensible as Brierly's, is moral suicide" (Moser, 42).

A year after Moser published his book on Conrad, Albert J. Guerard published *Conrad the Novelist.* Guerard went back to the idea of the double, not to stress that Jim is Conrad's double (as Morf had) or that Gentleman Brown is Jim's double (as both Morf and Van Ghent had) but, rather, to suggest that Marlow sees Jim as *his* double. Guerard thus implicitly agrees with Moser that Marlow is not just a narrator but also a perceptive hero. There is another notion in Moser's book, moreover, that Guerard expands on in his study of Conrad: the idea that *Lord Jim* implicates and involves the reader in interesting and positive ways, not only because of the way in which the story is told but also as a result of its ambiguities. (Early reviewers had spoken of the text's *obstructive* effect.)

Guerard points out, more clearly than Moser, the effect of the narrative structure on the reader. He explains that when Jim tells his story to Marlow, Marlow becomes like a reader—like us. When Marlow tells Jim's story to an audience, we are (and may consciously or subconsciously realize we are) like that audience. Finally, when Marlow tells his audience, which includes us, that Jim was "one of us," we identify more directly with Jim—and with Marlow in his identification with Jim—than we would were the story told by an omniscient narrator. "The reader," Guerard writes, "must . . . go through this labyrinth of evidence without the usual guide of an omniscient author or [even a] trustworthy author-surrogate." Guerard, however, sees the absence of an omniscient narrator, as well as the presence of a whole set of unreliable audience-guides, as a positive thing: it leads to what he calls a "delicate interplay of sympathy and judgement."[7]

Guerard, like Moser, suggests that it makes no sense, on the one hand, to think of the novel as an ambiguous text calling for the reader's discerning judgment and, on the other, to assume that what Stein says about "how to be" is equally Conrad's philosophy of life. "We cannot be sure of what Conrad thought about Stein," Guerard contends. Certainly, Stein "is not, unequivocally, a spokesman for the author" (Guerard, 90–91). Given the novel's structure, language, and attendant ambiguities, Guerard goes on to point out, we cannot even be entirely sure what Stein means. Whereas "the frequent reading" of " 'to the destructive element submit yourself' is *'man must learn to live with his unideal limitations,'"* it seems to Guerard that Stein's statement means just the opposite: man must immerse himself in ideal dreams even though they are the destructive element. Of the novel's two complementary "pendant characters" (by which Guerard means Stein and the French lieutenant), Stein is, after all, the "romantic."

In 1971 two books were published that, though generally in line with those studies which had viewed *Lord Jim* as a psychological and/or philosophical novel, took a somewhat different tack on the whole subject of mind and idea as they are present in literary texts.

Royal Roussel's *The Metaphysics of Darkness* took what has been referred to as a phenomenological approach to Conrad's fiction—an approach to literature based on the philosophy of Martin Heidegger and Edmund Husserl. Roussel begins his book with a fair summary of the aims of phenomenological criticism, announcing that his book "is an attempt to discover the unity" or "coherence" of "Conrad's fiction," the "fundamental vision at the center," the "central perception" that "generate[s] a world."[8] Calling his book an attempt to understand Conrad's "consciousness" by discovering patterns observable in all the writer's works, Roussel explains that he must begin by "intentionally ignor[ing] chronological order" and by talking about numerous works at once (Roussel, viii).

What Roussel finds consistent in Conrad's oeuvre is a concern with appearances: appearances that *seem* to reveal some reassuring deep truth (as the peaceful surface of the sea *seems* to suggest the peaceful nature of the cosmos to Jim) but that end up being at odds with a dark and formless reality. What Roussel also finds throughout Conrad's work are characters who respond to the apparent meaninglessness of the surrounding element by trying either to project an orderly and believable alternative world or to create such a world through language, "independent of the destructive force at the center of creation" (Roussel, 91). In *Lord Jim* Roussel finds these "central perceptions" in everything from Stein's statement about the need to immerse oneself in the dream to Marlow's statement that "words also belong to the sheltering conception of light and order which is our refuge" (Roussel, 90). But Roussel also finds them in Conrad's letters and even in conversational remarks attributed to Conrad, in which the author commented on art, chaos, and the need to control the latter via the former.

Like Roussel, Bruce Johnson considers *Conrad's Models of Mind* without resorting to Freudian or Jungian psychology for explanations of Conrad or his characters. Like Roussel, too, Johnson is interested in the way in which Conrad's characters desire to create their own world in response to an unexpectedly hostile one. At the end of *Lord Jim,* Johnson writes, "What we are left with is not the authority of fixed standards but the power of the human ego and imagination to confer value upon abstractions and to idealize its own desires. What matters isn't whether Jim's death is a triumph or not but that in his world it is."[9] Johnson relates Conrad's tendency to create heroes—especially white heroes—who imaginatively shape their own world to the Victorian belief that "the savage is one with nature, while the civilized white man has fallen from primal unity." Unlike the "native," who "feels no sense of alienation," the white colonist feels "the need to create his own contingent values and sanctions" (Johnson, 71–72).

Conrad's view of alienated people creating their own world, values, and sanctions, Johnson points out, anticipates the existential philosophy of Jean-Paul Sartre. "If we think in Sartre's terms it is clear that Jim undertakes Patusan in order more nearly to become God—not in the mundane sense of being worshipped by natives but as a man who seeks to enhance his own consciousness of his own being-in-itself" (Johnson, 92).

In *Conrad's Romanticism* (1974) David Thorburn interpreted *Lord Jim* in the context of literary rather than philosophical texts. Conrad's "young hero," Thorburn argues, "dragged unready into a world of moral and physical menace, is both a cliché of the adventure mode and a figure of seminal importance in Conrad's finest books."[10] But Thorburn is careful to show how Conrad artistically *modified* the adventure mode, experimenting with first-person narration to show how the mind of a young hero responds to the trials of experience.

Conrad, according to Thorburn, shows how his hero has been

matured by experience by having the adventurer recollect the adventure years later. By doing so, Conrad responds to the tradition of romantic poetry as well as that of the adventure story. "It is striking," Thorburn writes, "how closely Conrad's most characteristic works resemble what M. H. Abrams has identified as the greater Romantic lyric, a poetic form whose defining features are the play of memory across time and the juxtaposition of an older poet with his younger self" (Thorburn, 103). Thorburn goes on to say, "Conrad, like the English Romantic poets, holds to a meager but partly sustaining faith in the power of language to make sense of the world . . . , however imperfectly . . . 'I cannot paint / What then I was [Wordsworth writes].' But I will try and I will come close" (Thorburn, 127). Marlow thus has a "vocabulary of uncertainty," a stuttering diction and syntax that reveals but also pushes out at the limits of language. "In *Lord Jim,* as in *Heart of Darkness,*" writes Thorburn, "the famous adjectival insistence which has so disturbed [F. R.] Leavis and others is for the most part an essential aspect of the novel's meaning." Marlow's fuzzy and imprecise-seeming adjectives thus, in Thorburn's view, only "reinforce . . . his stated conviction that his telling must fall short of perfect truth" (Thorburn, 118).

Ian Watt had a somewhat different explanation for Conrad's language when he took up the question in his 1979 study of *Conrad in the Nineteenth Century.* Rather than relating it, as Thorburn does, to the romantic quest via poetry for the past and other impossibly elusive truths, Watt connects the ambiguity of Conrad to the impressionist movement—a movement we usually associate with painting, not literature. Although Watt says that Conrad's reactions to impressionist paintings were "predominantly unfavourable"[11] he goes on to say, speaking specifically of *Heart of Darkness,* that Conrad's style is "essentially impressionist" in that it presents experience subjectively, through the perceptions of narrators trying to decipher a world of apparently disconnected experiences (Watt, 174).

Just as characters in Conrad's novels see the world as we might see an impressionist painting—in "*Heart of Darkness*" Marlow first thinks the arrows raining down on him are "little sticks"—so we similarly experience the world *of* a Conrad novel. One of the reasons we do is Conrad's achronological style of presentation, that habit of separating chronologically contiguous events and juxtaposing ones far separated in time.

Watt, unlike the early reviewers of *Lord Jim,* sees "the achronological nature" of the novel as an artful part of Conrad's "impressionist narrative method" (Watt, 283). That Conrad tells us about Brierly's suicide just after Marlow's hospital visit with the alcoholic engineer "has nothing to do with chronology," Watt writes, yet it helps us to work through "moral analogies." We see great differences but also surprising similarities between men who would seem to represent opposite ends of the human spectrum. More important, the juxtaposition of the two scenes challenges us to wonder about the "moral problem" Jim may be unable to face (Watt, 280).

As (re)viewed by Watt, moreover, Conrad's achronological presentation is not just a matter of scrambling the order of major plot events. It is something that happens even at the level of the sentence—something that makes Conrad's style the ambiguous, demanding, but finally productive as well as poetical one that it is. "To describe [Conrad's] handling of time," Watt writes, "such terms as flashback or time shift suggest much too gross a calibration of temporal relationships. At the lowest order of magnitude, in the sequence of phrases and sentences in the narrative texture, Conrad's basic pattern is often comprised of a series of minute moves forwards and backwards in time" (Watt, 300).

With Watt's return to the subject of Conrad's achronology, it almost seems that criticism of *Lord Jim* has come full circle. And indeed, several major studies of Conrad written since 1980 re-cover old ground, though in new theoretical vehicles. Daniel Schwarz, in *Conrad: "Almayer's Folly" to "Under Western Eyes"* (1980), begins by expounding reader-response theory, which holds that readers collaborate with texts to produce meaning. But Schwarz ends up returning to the same issues that Gustav Morf and some of the original reviewers considered when writing about *Lord Jim.*

Schwarz pays considerable attention to the Gentleman Brown episode, arguing that "once Jim recognises a mirror image in [Brown], the social fabric he has woven on Patusan collapses."[12] Schwarz also sees Jim and Marlow as alter egos (Jim, though, is the "captive of his own imagination," whereas Marlow is "the rational empiricist"), arguing that the book depicts the "gradual movement of Jim towards Marlow's original position and the counter-movement of Marlow's towards Jim's" (Schwarz, 76). Where reader-response criticism allows Schwarz to break new ground is in leading him to imply that we, as readers, are changed by our interactions with the world of *Lord Jim,* much as Jim and Marlow, as a result of their interaction, move in one another's direction. This insight allows Schwarz to posit that "Marlow, like his creator, suggests the possibility of creating a community of understanding which he believes is the only possible replacement for a community based on moral standards" (Schwarz, 94).

Much as Schwarz uses newly fashioned theory to return to and develop some very old ideas, so Suresh Raval, best known for a book on poststructuralist critical theory, almost sounds like one of *Lord Jim*'s original reviewers when he passionately defends the Patusan episode of the novel, and in particular the parts involving Jewel. In his book on Conrad entitled *The Art of Failure* (1986), Raval reminds us that critics from F. R. Leavis to Raval's contemporary, the Marxist critic Fredric Jameson, have understood those parts to be a failure. (Jameson, in a difficult chapter on *Lord Jim* published in his provocative work *The Political Unconscious* [1981], refers to much of "the second half" of the novel as a "wish-fulfilling romance" and thus a "degraded narrative.")[13] In Raval's view, that perspective is too harsh; even the book's treatment of the relationship between Jewel and Jim does in fact reveal a great deal about Jim, for he "remains completely blind to the anxiety that attends her love. . . . Their love is defined by a lack of reciprocity in communication engendered primarily by Jim's . . . refusal to connect his past with his present."[14] The episodes involving Jim and Jewel, in Raval's view, thus show that "even before Brown's arrival, Jim remains tragically immersed in isolation and egoism" (Raval, 68).

Of course, criticism like history doesn't really come full circle; it only seems to. Underlying Raval's defense of the Patusan episode is an understanding of Marxist criticism that early reviewers didn't possess. Present-day new historicist critics are interested in Conrad's representation of the East not because it takes us to places faraway and blissfully romantic—which is why the original reviewers liked it—but, rather, because it shows us something about the literature of colonialism. Feminist critics have recently shown a renewed interest in the character of Jewel, not because they think her sweet and noble, as the earlier reviewers did, but because they are interested in what the text can tell us about Conrad's patriarchal culture's attitudes toward women—particularly women of color.

It almost seems, when we go from the first lines of the "General Prologue" to Chaucer's *Canterbury Tales* (concerning the way April's sweet showers awaken the birds and the bees and the human spirit as well) to the first lines of T. S. Eliot's *The Waste Land* ("April is the cruellest month, breeding / Lilacs out of the dead land") that literary history has come full circle. But, of course, it really hasn't: it came back to the same images and themes, but with a difference as vast as the one between medieval England and England after World War I. And so it is with the critical literature on *Lord Jim*. When literature comes around again, it comes around like a spring, moving outward and forward from the ideas of the past even as it seems to come back toward them again.

A Reading

4

The Fall: "I Had Jumped . . . It Seems"

A tragedy, Aristotle tells us, is the story of someone who falls from a high, noble position in society to a low, degraded one. We do not begin Conrad's *Lord Jim* knowing that we are reading a modern tragedy, but we can hardly help suspecting, from the novel's title alone, that the protagonist of the story we are about to read is either well born or, at least, aristocratic by nature or temperament. "Lord" Jim, we are likely to infer, will turn out to be someone in control, someone to whom others look for leadership, direction, and support.

The first paragraph of the novel at once rewards and defeats our expectation. The character introduced by the narrator, the "he" referred to by the novel's first word, has a commanding voice, is tall and "powerfully built," and "walks straight at you," to be sure. But he also walks with a "slight stoop of the shoulders, head forward, and a fixed-from-under stare which made you think of a charging bull." He is characterized by self-assertion, but it is a "dogged self-assertion," a kind of insistent, aggressive quality that seems to compensate for the lack of something else (3).

The character we meet in the novel's opening paragraph goes about his duties as a water clerk dressed spectacularly "from shoes to hat" (3). But why, we can hardly help wondering, is a man dressed so splendidly working as a supplier of ships in Far Eastern ports? Something must have dragged him down, for he seems a character meant for a better life than the one he is leading. Something must have "stooped" the shoulders of one otherwise tall and powerful. The image of the "charging bull," after all, elicits in the reader's mind—the mind of the "you" addressed by the narrator—the complementary image of the matador, the almost-inevitable victor of the bullfight, the one who is goading unfairly his noble opponent, provoking a deadly battle the bull is most unlikely to win. Who or what, we may wonder, is goading the "he" of the first paragraph, making his acts of self-assertion "dogged," enforcing a lowlife far from Europe that is somehow at odds with his dress, his bearing, and his voice?

The narrator incites such questions but at first will not answer them, except insofar as to let us know we are right to think there is *something* that causes this water clerk "apparelled in" the "immaculate white" befitting a nobleman on safari to live incognito in place after place (3). "When the fact broke through the incognito," the narrator tells us, "Jim would leave suddenly the seaport where he happened to be at the time and go to another—generally farther east" (4). But the narrator is slow to tell us what that fact, that something, *is* that drives Jim from job to job, island to island, farther and farther from where he started out. At first he will only give that fact a maddeningly unspecific name. It was "the Intolerable," we are told. Or, rather, we are told that it was Jim's "keen perception of the Intolerable" that "drove him away for good" from one location after another (5).

In the paragraph after the one in which we are teased with such a baffling definition of Jim's nemesis, we are given information about his background. Jim's father is a rector of the Church of England—one possessing "certain knowledge" not of the "Intolerable" but, rather, of God, whom the narrator wryly calls "the Unknowable" (5). That the narrator speaks of the minister as one with knowledge of what cannot be known is a point we should not overlook. It prepares us for what follows: a passage in which Britain's class system is implicitly but pointedly interrogated.

The Fall: "I Had Jumped . . . It Seems"

The knowledge disseminated by Jim's father is of such a kind "as made for the righteousness of people in cottages without disturbing the ease of mind of those whom an unerring Providence enables to live in mansions." Not a "lord" himself, Jim's father is nonetheless on the inside of something ancient and powerful. He lives in a rectory that, though not quite a "mansion," glows "with a warm tint in the midst of grass-plots, flower beds, and fir-trees, with an orchard at the back, a paved stable yard to the left, and the sloping glass of greenhouses." What he has, he has inherited, just as noblemen inherit property: "The living had belonged to the family for generations" (5). It is little wonder that Jim's father preaches of an "unerring Providence," a Lord *of* lords who enables people to inherit and idly live in mansions, their "ease of mind undisturbed."

Because of his father's vocation, Jim would have been a likely candidate for admission to Oxford or Cambridge had he wanted to take up the family "living" by entering the ministry. But he "was one of five children" and, apparently, the one least likely to pursue such a course. His calling was the sea; his vocation was not, therefore, to be a man of the Lord but, rather, to be an officer and a gentleman. "When after a course of light holiday literature his vocation for the sea had declared itself, he was sent at once to a 'training-ship for officers of the mercantile marine'" (5).

As we have seen in the passage concerning "knowledge" of the "Unknowable," the narrator of the opening chapters of *Lord Jim* plants subtle hints that can guide our response to the narrative. Although we do not yet have the remotest idea why a tall, well-dressed Englishman with a powerful voice is in Eastern ports selling candles and water to ship captains, we may detect a hint of Jim's tragic flaw in what we are told about the motivation for his maritime career. Despite the fact that we are not to learn, for several chapters, why Jim runs from wherever it is he is making his meager living as soon as his surname becomes known, we can imagine how someone might fall from high to low, from a noble to an ignoble identity, by making "light holiday literature" the grounds for going off to sea.

To decide on being an officer of the merchant marine just because one finds tales of adventure exhilarating is to fail to first see whether the reality of the sailing life corresponds to its fictional representations. More important, to launch into such a life without considering whether one's inner qualities match those of real or fictional maritime heroes is to show lack of self-knowledge or even the desire for it. And, as readers of tragedies from Sophocles's *Oedipus Rex* onward know, a reluctance to learn or an inability to see the truth, especially about oneself, is a characteristic held in common by countless tragic heroes who fall as low in life as they begin high.

That Jim has long been blind to reality, including and perhaps especially his own inner reality, is strongly suggested by the paragraphs chronicling his education on the training ship. At first, there is no reason for Jim to suspect that a gap exists between self-image and what, for lack of a better term, we may call self-reality. For a while, nothing happens to contradict his sense that his character is as lofty as his "station" on the training ship. From his vantage point "in the fore-top," he looks "down" onto the busy deck with all "the contempt of a man destined to shine in the midst of dangers." Later, when down on the "lower deck in the babel of two hundred voices he would forget himself, and beforehand live in his mind the sea-life of light literature" (6). For a while, then, he is able rationally to assume that he is destined for figurative as well as literal heights: "He saw himself saving people from sinking ships, cutting away masts in a hurricane, swimming through a surf with a line, or as a lonely castaway, barefooted and half naked, walking on uncovered reefs in search of shellfish to stave off starvation. He confronted savages on tropical shores, quelled mutinies on the high seas, and in a small boat upon the ocean kept up the hearts of despairing men—always an example of devotion to duty, and as unflinching as a hero in a book" (6). Suddenly, though, something happens—something as unexpected as the collision of the *Patna,* that later something, event, or "fact" that has led to Jim's tragic fall.

Called from below onto a gale-swept deck, Jim discovers that "a coaster running for shelter had crashed through a schooner at anchor." A "mob of boys" eager to help people hurt in the accident "clambered on the rails" of the training ship, hoping to be lowered in the cutter designed for use in just such an emergency. Suddenly Jim is "whirled around," probably by the wind; then he is "jostled," probably by an eager schoolmate. "A push" next makes him "stagger against the mizzen-mast, and he caught hold of a rope." The delays—or so he later seems to have convinced himself—prevent him from doing what the other boys do, namely, rescue two drowning men. "Jim felt his shoulder gripped firmly. 'Too late, youngster.' . . . The captain smiled sympathetically. 'Better luck next time. This will teach you to be smart'" (7–8).

Rather than wondering self-critically whether he is cut out for the life led so ably and enthusiastically by the other boys—the boys whose behavior has approximated that of his literary heroes—Jim diminishes what his peers have done. He turns the fact that they have overcome the elements into evidence that the elements weren't all that threatening, that they were, after all, an "inefficient menace. Now he knew what to think of . . . the gale. He could affront greater perils. He would do so—better than anybody" (8).

It is true that Jim ends up "brood[ing] apart that evening while the bowman of the cutter—a boy with a face like a girl's and big grey eyes—was the hero of the lower deck": "Eager questioners crowded round [the bowman]. He narrated: 'I just saw his head bobbing, and I dashed my boathook in the water. It caught in his breeches and I nearly went overboard, as I thought I would, only old Symons let go the tiller and grabbed my legs—the boat nearly swamped'" (8). But Jim quickly gets over his brooding, not by coming to appreciate and help celebrate what the boy and "old Symons" have managed to accomplish but, rather, by diminishing their deeds in his mind, just as he had earlier diminished the storm. He "thought it a pitiful display of vanity. The gale had ministered to a heroism as spurious as its own pretence of terror." Jim even comes to feel happy that he had not had time to get into the cutter. Since "a lower achievement had served the turn" of saving the two men's lives, his own efforts had not been needlessly wasted. "When all men flinched, then—he felt sure—he alone would know how to deal with the spurious menace of wind and seas" (9).

The passage quoted at length above, the boy whose heroic efforts are described therein, and the character of the boy's language are deserving of close attention. They anticipate a later passage, one devoted to a French captain who does on the *Patna* what Jim hadn't the nerve to do. Like that French captain whom he anticipates, the young "hero of the *lower* deck" (emphasis added) practices a form of discourse that is entirely without the high, poetic flourishes we might expect from a hero—particularly from "a hero in a book" (6).

Jim's audacious characterization of the boy's humble and straightforward (we might say "down-to-sea") language as "a pitiful display of vanity" can be seen as Conrad's way of showing us that Jim himself is a victim of vanity or pride. And pride, as we know, has gone before a fall ever since pride went before *the* Fall, the Fall of humankind from Paradise that resulted from the overreaching of Adam and Eve for an identity and state in which God had not created them. The vanity implicit in Jim's characterizing as vanity the "narrat[ion]" of the "below-decks hero" foreshadows Jim's fall on—and from—the *Patna*.

I began this discussion by suggesting that *Lord Jim* is not unlike a Greek tragedy, that the protagonist is a tragic hero, and that the hero's fall from high to low is caused by an almost-willful refusal to seek knowledge—especially knowledge about whether or not his own nature corresponds to the idealized nature he has encountered in romantic adventure tales. But Jim's fall can also be seen as the result of pride, instead of (or as well as) being seen as the result of a refusal to seek knowledge. Viewed this way, the biblical story of the Fall, instead of (or in addition to) a Greek tragedy like *Oedipus Rex*, is analogous to *Lord Jim*. The seductive literature Jim has read—the romantic texts that have encouraged him to think of himself as being above other human beings—might even be seen as the analog to the words of the original tempter, the Serpent in the Garden of Eden who encouraged Adam and Eve to think of themselves as being on the level of God.

If we were to see as prototypes for Conrad's novel *both* the biblical story of the Fall *and* the fall of the tragic hero, we would need to respond to an objection that can easily be raised. We would need to explain that, whereas the biblical Fall is precipitated by Adam and Eve's eating of the fruit of the Tree of Knowledge, Jim's fall, when viewed as that of a tragic hero, would appear to have been precipitated by a *lack* of knowledge—more precisely, by a lack of self-knowledge. Our explanation might begin with the observation that Jim's tragic innocence about his own nature is hardly comparable to the simple innocence of Adam and Eve before the Fall. Indeed, Jim's innocence can be seen as a form of pride, for it results from his refusal to accept—from an unwillingness to swallow—the bitter fact that he was never cut out to be a hero.

In chapter 2 Jim goes to sea, this time as a sailor and not as a student. And for some time, all goes reassuringly—just as it did for a while on the training ship. Having become an officer and entered "the regions so well known to his imagination," Jim is allowed by events, or the lack thereof, to continue thinking of himself as he has thought of himself all along—the inconvenient gale notwithstanding. He is measured merely by his "knowledge of his duties," which, because it is "thorough," causes him to be made "chief mate of a fine ship" while he is still a very young man. Politically, his position is high above that of the other sailors, just as physically it was above that of the boys "below decks" when he stood "in the fore-top" of the training ship and "looked down, with the contempt of a man destined to shine in the midst of dangers."

But Jim, we sense, is highly vulnerable. We sense this because of the way in which the narrator opens the chapter. He makes a point of the fact that the new chief mate has never "been tested by those events of the sea that show in the light of day the inner worth of a man, the edge of his temper, and the fibre of his stuff; that reveal the quality of his resistance and the secret truth of his pretences, not only to others but also to himself" (10). Spared the knowledge of that truth referred to earlier as "the secret truth of his pretences," Jim is able to remain a little longer where he has been living for so long, namely, in a world of the imagination in which he is—or soon will be—a hero to eclipse all others. The reader, however, has been conditioned by the narrator's comments to suspect that that world is an illusion, a fool's paradise Jim refused to be shaken from on the day when a gale nearly drowned two men—and a very brave boy.

When, a page or so into chapter 2, a second, unexpected storm blows up to test Jim's mettle a second time—to suggest something about his inner worth, the edge of his temper, the fiber of his stuff—the reader is as unsurprised as Jim is caught off guard. Nor does it comes as a surprise, to the reader, that Jim just happens to be unable, once again, to be in life what he is in the "regions so well known to his imagination." He is "disabled by a falling spar at the beginning of a week of which his Scottish captain used to say afterwards, 'Man! it's a pairfect meeracle to me how she lived through it!'" (11).

This time, Jim does seem to entertain the possibility that his injury is some kind of outward manifestation of an unacceptable, inner fear. He "spent many days stretched on his back, dazed, battered, hopeless, and tormented as if at the bottom of an abyss of unrest." It is as if his dream-prone, romantic imagination, which has long represented him to himself as a swashbuckling hero afraid of nothing, now torments him with an alternative image of cowardice. But the sense of danger, felt keenly on deck, slowly abates below. Soon Jim becomes "secretly glad he had not had to go on deck"—just as earlier he had become secretly glad that he had not had to waste his energies saving two men capable of being saved by "a boy with a face like a girl's." Before long he has recovered from his fear and, more significantly, from his fear that his nature may be fearful. The "fine weather returned, and he thought no more about it" (11). Left behind by his ship to completely recover, he eventually ships out as chief mate on the fateful *Patna.*

The *Patna,* we can hardly fail to note, is a ship carrying no ordinary cargo. "Owned by a Chinaman, chartered by an Arab," the ship is carrying "pilgrims," Moslems from the Far East making a journey of faith, back to the source of their beliefs in the Middle East, presumably Mecca. "They streamed aboard over three gangways, they streamed in urged by faith and the hope of paradise." They had come to board the *Patna* "from north and south and from the outskirts of the East, after treading the jungle paths, descending the rivers":

> At the call of an idea they had left their forests, their clearings, the protection of their rulers, their prosperity, their poverty, the surroundings of their youth and the graves of their fathers. They came

> covered with dust, with sweat, with grime, with rags—the strong men at the head of family parties, the lean old men pressing forward without hope of return; young boys with fearless eyes glancing curiously, shy little girls with tumbled long hair; the timid women muffled up and clasping to their breasts, wrapped in loose ends of soiled head-cloths, their sleeping babies, the unconscious pilgrims of an exacting belief. (14–15)

In spite of the fact that they are transporting "human cargo," in spite of the fact that even the youngest passengers are setting into the unknown "fearless[ly]" out of "belief" in an "idea," the white men of Western European descent in charge of the *Patna* and its cargo are hardly prone to treat the dark-skinned pilgrims of another faith with an overabundance of respect. Indeed, in the eyes of the captain of the *Patna,* these seekers of "paradise" are not even *human* cargo: "'Look at dese cattle,' said the German skipper to [Jim,] his new chief mate" (15). "The five whites on board lived amidships," the narrator tells us, "isolated" by choice from their living load (16). Collectively, the officers of the *Patna* feel far above the level of the people they are transporting. They feel as far above them as people feel they are above animals fit for slaughter, as far above them as not a few English lords have felt they are above cottagers, as far above the mass of humanity below decks as Jim feels he is above "all" other "men"—men who will "flinch" on the day he alone will "know how to deal" with an otherwise insuperable "menace."

The pride of the officers, as revealed by the captain's characterization of the Easterners as "cattle," repeats the pride of Jim, who had earlier revealed his vanity by feeling "contempt" for the "babel" of the training ship's "lower deck." It similarly foreshadows a fall: the fall to be suffered when the officers yield to the temptation to jump ship and perhaps a greater, more significant lapse as well. The pride of the officers, in light of their subsequent conduct, may foreshadow the fall of Western idealism, the belief in what the novel later calls "standard[s] of conduct" (50).

At the heart of Western culture, even back in the times when Greek tragedies were written, has been the belief that human nature is such that individuals may reasonably be *expected* to put others' needs ahead of their own, to sacrifice self for the greater common good. At the heart of the Judeo-Christian faith, the faith that has informed Western culture since the waning of Greece, is belief in God's law or commandments and Christ's "new" law of self-sacrifice. The fall adumbrated by the captain's proud characterization of the pilgrims as "cattle" is one that throws into question whether human beings *will* uphold the law when under extreme duress, *will* give up their own lives for the sake of others.

The event that triggers this fall is as sudden and therefore unanticipated as were those earlier gales that demanded a brave and unselfconcerned response by Jim. Up until the shock of the accident is felt, the ship's passage seems as smooth and perfect to the officers as Jim's passage through life seems to Jim. If Jim were a careful *reader* of his life, of course, he might see in it subtle but sinister evidence that, though all seems well, a crisis lies ahead, just as if we are careful readers of Conrad's text, we might see tumultuous trouble foreshadowed in the very language that tells us just how quiet and calm the sea was. Note that the word *hiss* alone, in the passage that follows, suggests that somewhere, somehow, there is danger in this paradise of tranquility. And the word *hiss* is but one of many words that suggests some kind of trouble lies ahead: "And under the sinister splendour of that sky the sea, blue and profound, remained still, without a stir, without a ripple, without a wrinkle—viscous, stagnant, dead. The *Patna,* with a slight hiss, passed over that plain luminous and smooth, unrolled a black ribbon of smoke across the sky, left behind her on the water a white ribbon of foam that vanished at once, like the phantom of a track drawn upon a lifeless sea by the phantom of a steamer" (15–16). But Jim is not a careful reader of the outer or inner world. "Jim on the bridge was penetrated by the great certitude of unbounded safety and peace that could be read on the silent aspect of nature." While he so reads the text of the world, we read it differently by attending to the small details of the text in which nature's text is represented by Conrad: "The propeller turned without a check, *as though* its beat had been part of the scheme of a safe universe; and on each side of the *Patna* two deep folds of water, permanent and somber on the unwrinkled shimmer, enclosed within their straight and diverging ridges a few white swirls of foam bursting *in a low hiss* (17; emphasis added). Later, our sense that Jim's reading of "unbounded safety and peace" in nature's silence is vindicated by an image even less ambiguous than phrases like "low hiss" and "as though . . . safe," namely, the symbolic image conveyed by the phrase "the shadow": "[Jim's] eyes roaming about the line of the horizon, seemed to gaze hungrily into the unattainable, and did not see the shadow of the coming event. The only shadow on the sea was the shadow of the black smoke pouring heavily from the funnel its immense streamer" (19).

Conrad is a genius at representing a world through images that are at once arrestingly realistic and also pregnant with suggestive and even symbolic value. The shadow of the smoke across an otherwise-blue sea is one example. An even better one is the cause of the "coming event" foretold by the shadow, namely, the barely floating, abandoned wreck of a ship, a "floating derelict" that would be barely visible by day and entirely invisible at night (159). The floating derelict is at once a believable cause of an accident, a telling image of what the *Patna* will soon be (that is, an abandoned wreck), and a powerful symbol suggestive of several ideas or themes of *Lord Jim*. It even turns out to be, in the long run, a foreshadowing itself of another floating or drifting derelict, Gentleman Brown, whose unexpected arrival on Patusan will later contribute as surely to Jim's final fall as the drifting derelict of the floating wreck contributes to his definitive tragic fall.

That the floating derelict is the believable cause of an accident at sea and an image of what the *Patna* literally becomes is a proposition too obvious to need defending; that it is a foreshadowed event that itself foreshadows an unanticipated, drifting human derelict is a notion to be explored in a later chapter of this study. What is important to realize, at this point, is how beautifully the image of the floating derelict symbolizes several themes already evident, both in the novel and, at least implicitly, in the foregoing discussion of it.

For one thing, the floating derelict serves as a reminder of the vulnerability we try to forget about—that is, the vulnerability of the human condition that gives powerful credibility to the tragic genre. No time of life, no period of history, is so untroubled that it cannot be interrupted by an unexpected crisis. This fragility of existence is one of several ideas that the floating derelict makes us think about, at least unconsciously.

Most vulnerable of all, of course, are those characters who so (foolishly) believe in themselves and their own indestructibility that they do not even keep on the lookout for dangers, the most dangerous of which will be hard to spot—and most dangerous precisely *because* they are so easy to miss. And of all the dangers human beings can remain blind to, their own faults are among the most difficult to see and, therefore, potentially tragic. The floating derelict, in addition to symbolizing the unexpected hitch that may undo any person's (or nation's or culture's) life, thus at the same time suggests the hidden or repressed dangers within ourselves—ourselves as individuals, as nations, or even as a species.

Jim can generally represent the tendency of human groups to be blind to their own faults because he, as an individual, epitomizes through his thoughts and actions the failure to acquire or accept self-knowledge. A passage like the following one exemplifies Jim's tendency to overlook his true inner nature (while writing a fictional one based on tales of heroism he has read):

> "How steady she goes," thought Jim with wonder, with something like gratitude for this high peace of sea and sky. At such times his thoughts would be full of valorous deeds: he loved these dreams and the success of his imaginary achievements. They were the best parts of life, its *secret truth*, its *hidden reality*. They had a gorgeous virility, the charm of vagueness, they passed before him with a heroic tread; they carried his soul away with them and made it drunk with the divine philtre of an unbounded confidence in itself. There was nothing he could not face. (20; emphasis added)

But as the "hidden reality" of the floating derelict reveals, Jim's hidden reality—the "secret truth" about his nature—is not "unbounded confidence." Nor is it "gorgeous virility"; nor is it an uncheckable will to do "valorous deeds." Nor does valor, virility, or confidence make up the hidden reality of European machismo as represented by the other officers on board the *Patna.* The as-yet-unwitnessed reality of their natures, rather, is what the derelict reveals it to be; more precisely, it is what the derelict *is,* dereliction being defined as culpable neglect, abandonment of duty, the act of abandoning. The nature revealed by the derelict hidden in darkness is the tendency toward dereliction that comes out of hiding when the *Patna* strikes a floating wreck.

Another strikingly suggestive image Conrad develops through his story of the *Patna*'s accident is that of the rusty plates forming the bulkhead of the old ship's forehold. We are first introduced to this image by a conversation between the German captain and the second engineer, a conversation that takes place just before the ship strikes the floating derelict. Accused of drunkenness by his superior, the second engineer responds by defending his own bravery, as if it were cowardice his captain had accused him of: "'I don't know what fear is,' pursued the engineer. . . . 'And a jolly good thing for you that there are some of us about the world that aren't afraid of their lives, or where would you be—you and this old thing here with her plates like brown paper—brown paper, s'elp me?'" (25).

It is just then—while the engineer lets go of the rail and makes "ample gestures as if demonstrating the . . . extent of his valour"—that Jim and the captain are staggered by something happening far below them: "What had happened? The wheezy thump of the engines went on. Had the earth been checked in her course? They could not understand; and suddenly the calm sea, the sky without a cloud, appeared formidably insecure in their immobility, as if poised on the brow of yawning destruction. . . . A faint noise as of thunder . . . passed slowly, and the ship thundered in response, as if the thunder had growled deep down in the water. . . . The sharp hull driving on its way seemed to rise a few inches through its whole length" (26). Told to "call no one and to make no noise for fear of creating a panic," Jim takes a lamp, opens a hatch, hears the telltale sound of splashing, and discovers the forepeak to be "half full of water already" (29). On realizing that the only thing separating the forepeak from the critical forehold area is that "collision bulkhead" just described as a collection of "plates like brown paper," Jim comes upon the author of the description, who has been in the forehold to survey the extent of the damage. "My God!" the second engineer exclaims. "That rotten bulkhead'll give way in a minute, and the damned thing will go down under us like a lump of lead" (30).

Jim's eventual abandonment of the *Patna* may have something to do with the fact that his experience of the strange, sudden rumbling below deck had been preceded by the second engineer's almost-certainly drunken, and perhaps somewhat exaggerated, account of rusty bulkhead plates like sheets of brown paper. Surely, the fact that he heard the plates described that way just before the accident—and then heard them called "rotten" just after the collision—is one of the reasons he went below to see the bulkhead for himself. And the sight of the plates is one of the reasons he gives later, at the inquiry into the incident, for abandoning a ship with 800 helpless, sleeping pilgrims on board.

As Jim later tells Marlow, who comes to know him through the inquiry and to tell his tale many times thereafter, a rusty plate was high on his list of reasons for jumping off the *Patna* and thereby falling from social respectability. "If you had stuck to the ship," Marlow offers at one point, to which Jim replies a few sentences later, "Dash it all! I tell you it bulged. I was holding up my lamp along the angle-iron when a flake of rust as big as the palm of my hand fell off the plate, all of itself. . . . The thing stirred and jumped off like something alive while I was looking at it" (84). At another point, Jim is even more passionate in his attempt to make Marlow believe that, had *he* seen the bulkhead, he, too, would have jumped. "Have you watched a ship floating head down, checked in sinking by a sheet of old iron too rotten to stand being shored up. Have you?" He proceeds without waiting for a response. "O yes, shored up? I thought of that— . . . but can you shore up a bulkhead in five minutes—or in fifty for that matter? Where was I going to get the . . . timber! Would you have had the courage to swing the maul for the first blow if you had seen that bulkhead? Don't say you would: you had not seen it; nobody would" (92).

Marlow, who comes to identify with Jim, can understand how the sight of a huge flake of rust popping off a paper-thin bulkhead might cause an officer to abandon a ship with hundreds of passengers and very few lifeboats. Or so it would seem from the sympathetic way in which he seems to describe Jim's actions when he tells Jim's story, many years later:

> You must remember he believed, as any other man would have done in his place, that the ship would go down at any moment; the bulging, rust-eaten plates that kept back the ocean, fatally must give way, all at once like an undermined dam, and let in a sudden and overwhelming flood. He stood still looking at these recumbent bodies, a doomed man aware of his fate, surveying the silent company of the dead. They *were* dead! Nothing could save them! . . .
>
> "Somebody was speaking aloud in my head," he said a little wildly. "Eight hundred people and seven boats—and no time! Just think of it." He leaned toward me across the little table, and I tried to avoid his stare. "Do you think I was afraid of death?" he asked in a voice very fierce and low. He brought down his open hand with a bang that made the coffee-cups dance. "I am ready to swear I was not. . . . By God–no!" (86–87)

What is it, then, that the rusty bulkhead plates symbolize or suggest, in addition to the simple plot element that they so obviously fulfill? For one thing, they can be read as evidence of the flimsiness of the self-image with which Jim holds back the terrible truth about himself. That self-image, which has miraculously survived the elements twice—first on the training ship that Jim imperiously lorded over and next on the ship whose "falling spar" disabled him—is not to survive the onrush of *these* seas, anymore than he would like to believe any other man's self-image would. "You think me a cur for standing there, but what would you have done?" he asked Marlow, just after insisting that Marlow would have made the same decision he made: not to try to shore up the bulkhead (92).

To the extent that Jim's early faith in his own heroic identity represents Western culture's faith in a particular idea or ideal, the bulkhead composed of flaky brown plates can also be read as a symbol of something broader than Jim's romantic and idealistic self-image. It can simultaneously be interpreted as a symbol of the flimsiness—better yet, the "rottenness"—of the idealistic self-image of his whole culture. That self-image, encoded as it is in what the novel calls the cultural "standard of conduct," is what seems to be breaking down, falling apart, as a group of officers who have been found exemplary enough to be certified after an appropriate testing and training period leave 800 souls to perish rather than waking them up and risking their own demise. Symbolically speaking, Western idealism in general and the heroic ideal in particular seem to be caving in under the pressures of historical events that expose their fraudulence and that, consequently, they cannot withstand.

But there is still another, almost-contradictory way to read the rusty plates. They can also be seen as representing the misleading nature of evidence and, by extension, the difficulty of "reading" the world and whatever forces, physical or metaphysical, are driving it. (Recall that the novel refers to the God of whom Jim's father pretends "knowledge" as the "Unknowable"; the bulging bulkhead plate is a striking symbol of that cosmic unknowability which lies behind so many great tragedies.) I have referred to this reading as being "almost contradictory" because, to the extent that the plates represent those things which are *not* crumbling—those which only appear to be rotten—they may suggest that everything from Jim's heroic identity to Western idealism may only *appear* to be rotten and shattering as Jim and his fellow officers jump from the Patna.

Whether or not the symbolism of the *apparently* rotten bulkhead extends so far as to suggest that Jim's or our culture's (or even our human) self-definition is only *apparently* flimsy or rotten is a question we will return to in future chapters. Suffice it to say, at this point, that the rusty bulkhead plates serve as a symbol of the world's unreadability. Once Jim mistakenly thought that "unbounded safety and peace . . . could be read on the silent aspect" that "nature" had manifested just before the accident. He failed at that point to "see," in the narrator's words, "the shadow of the coming event." When the "event"—the collision—happens, Jim once again misreads his surroundings, for he sees in a "bulging, rust-eaten plate," and more specifically in a popping rust flake the size of his hand, "the shadow of

[a] coming event" that never comes, namely, the event of the *Patna*'s sinking. Like the second engineer, he sees a bulging bulkhead and interprets it to mean that "the damned thing will go down under us like a lump of lead" (30).

The *Patna,* of course, mysteriously or "unknowably"—and at the same time just naturally—fails to "go down." ("At about nine o'clock the next morning," a French gunboat comes upon the still-floating steamer, with "decks . . . packed as close as a sheep pen," with "people perched all along the rails" (136–37). What fails, gives way, and goes down turns out to be not the decrepit boat but, rather, the officers who are supposedly commanding it. First they descend in dignity from the level at which their positions—and their corresponding self-images—would indicate they should be, becoming exactly like the pilgrims they assume would, if awakened, become "clamorous with distress" (86). The ship's officers descend, in other words, from what they have been in their minds, namely, human beings above the level of other human beings, to a level of mere humanity seldom written about in adventure tales. The second engineer, Jim tells the court of inquiry, "pushed me away with his right arm and ran before me up the ladder, shouting as he climbed. . . . I followed him in time to see the captain rush at him and knock him flat on his back. . . . I fancy he was asking him why the devil he didn't stop the engines, instead of making a row about it on deck. I heard him say, 'Get up! Run! fly!' He swore also" (30).

Next they descend in behavior and dignity to a level below that of mere humanity. They stoop below, in fact, the level of conduct that officers carrying nonhuman cargo might expect of "sheep," which is what Jim has figuratively called the pilgrims, or "cattle," the term used by the skipper. Jim has secretly felt above the other officers ever since joining the ship as chief mate ("he rubbed shoulders with them, but they could not touch him; he shared the air they breathed, but he was different"; 24–25). But the moment in which, lantern in hand, he reaches the deck on which the *Patna*'s few lifeboats are stored reveals that he is unable not to sink, along with them, to a condition of existence below that of pacific animals. It is then that one of the pilgrims who has been sleeping outside in the cool awakens and catches hold of Jim's coat as he runs by. Jim initially gives a jerk to get away but then feels the pilgrim's arm embracing his leg: "'The beggar clung to me like a drowning man,'" [Jim] said, impressively. '"Water, water!" What water did he mean? What did he know? As calmly as I could I ordered him to let go. He was stopping me, time was pressing, other men began to stir; I wanted time—time to cut the boats adrift. He got hold of my hand now, and I felt that he would begin to shout. It flashed upon me it was enough to start a panic, and I hauled off with my free arm and slung the lamp in his face'" (90). The boy who once felt he would act nobly "when all men flinched" now acts like a savage animal, a "cur," to use a term he himself uses in a passage quoted earlier. He injures a man who turns out to need water not just for himself but for a "sick" and "thirsty" child (90).

Soon all the officers are turning into animals, turning on anyone and everyone who might seem to pose a threat to their escape, including one another. Jim is hammered with "a heavy blow," delivered with a tool used to get the boats off the chocks, by none other than the *Patna*'s chief engineer. "Somehow I had no mind to be surprised," Jim later tells Marlow. "All this seemed natural—and awful—and awful. I dodged that miserable maniac, lifted him off the deck . . . , and he started whispering in my arms: *'Don't! Don't! I thought you were one of the niggers.'* I flung him away, he skidded along the bridge and knocked the legs from under the little chap, the second [engineer]. The skipper, busy about the boat, looked round and came at me head down, *growling like a wild beast.* I flinched no more than a stone. . . . I drew back my fist and he stopped short, muttering—'Ah! it's you. Lend a hand quick'" (91). The irony of men who are "growling like wild beasts" apologizing with phrases like "I thought you were one of the niggers" is too sharp to go unfelt. It is only deepened a few pages later when the captain urges Jim to hurry up and help clear the boat because he won't "get the ghost of a show" if all those "brutes" awaken and manage to "get in the water" (103).

Jim makes a brief, last effort to reestablish his difference, thereby resurrecting his old sense of a noble identity. "There was nothing to do but sink with the ship," he says to himself (99). He may have swung a lantern in a man's face, but he is surely not such a "wild beast" as those who would jump like rats from a boat going down. But then he seems to become confused in his values, on hearing the chief engineer ask him, "Won't you save your own life—you infernal coward?" Is it possible, Jim wonders, that a coward would be someone who would remain behind, *afraid* to leap out into the blackness? Then too, another unexpected thing happens. Jim sees the third engineer, who is just stepping into the lifeboat, "step backwards suddenly, clutch at the air with raised arms, totter and collapse" (107). The boat is lowered and shoved off just as Jim, still on deck, watches the third engineer die. "Jump, George! We'll catch you! Jump!" the men yell from below, thinking the man they see poised at the edge of the deck is their third engineer. Jim isn't George, but in that moment he is no better than George—in fact, he is worse if George's collapse and death were somehow precipitated by a crisis of conscience. Like three other officers who have suddenly become "wild beasts," he falls a distance far greater than the one from the deck of the *Patna* to the ocean's surface. As Jim puts it, "I had jumped . . . it seems. . . . It was as if I had jumped into a well—into an everlasting deep hole" (111). Marlow phrases it slightly differently, foreshadowing much of the action of the novel to come: "He had tumbled from a height he could never scale again" (112).

5

After the Fall: The Inquiries

As every reader of *Lord Jim* knows, the second quarter of the book, roughly speaking, concerns an "Inquiry" into the actions taken by Jim and the three other officers who abandoned the *Patna*. The inquiry is of significance to the novel—not just to *Lord Jim* in particular but to fiction as a genre—for the novel is essentially a moral form, as Wayne Booth has argued in *The Rhetoric of Fiction*. This is not to say that it is a moral*istic* form; indeed, any novel that hits us over the head with moral maxims is considered an inferior example of what the novel can and should do. Rather, it is to say that novels, unlike lyric poems, are almost inevitably about moral or ethical issues. Like the epic that came before it, the novel presents characters, sometimes heroes, being tested by other characters and by circumstances. But unlike those epics in which the test may only be one of endurance, cleverness, or even sexual prowess, novels from *Clarissa* to *Lord Jim* almost always represent protagonists or heroes who are morally on trial.

When we read a poem like Wallace Stevens's "Sunday Morning" or Keats's "Ode on a Grecian Urn," we are obviously not looking for "good guys and bad guys." Neither are we doing anything so simple as what we do when we read novels like Stephen Crane's *The Red*

Badge of Courage or Theodore Dreiser's *Sister Carrie.* Nonetheless, we *are* asking questions about ethics. Is the central character in Stephen Crane's novel merely a coward? Or does his running from war signal that his is a higher morality? Is Sister Carrie forced by circumstance and environment to participate in crime? Or is there a flaw in her character as well?

Thus, the domination of the second quarter of *Lord Jim* by a formal inquisition into character—into why four men did what they did and what, if anything, ought to be the punishment for it—is perfectly natural and appropriate to the novel form. In a way, all readers of all novels are busy conducting quiet investigations of their own, anyway. The process of reading fiction, dominated as fiction is by questions of "character" (the word itself has a double, moral connotation), is essentially that of conducting an inquiry. And, as readers, we take our lead from the characters whose "character" we are ever inquiring into. The heroes and heroines of most novels, like Conrad's Jim, are conducting inquiries into past and present reality, including their own inner reality, with the goal of knowledge and self-knowledge.

As the title of this chapter suggests, though, there is not one but, rather, several inquiries going on in the second quarter of *Lord Jim.* There is, of course, the formal inquiry involving the officers of the *Patna,* a magistrate, two assessors, and a packed courtroom. But this is in some ways a less interesting inquiry than the one the narrator-character Marlow decides to conduct on his own. Having heard the testimony given at the formal inquiry, Marlow makes a point over a period of days, weeks, and years to interview characters who can bear witness to Jim, what he did, and what happened. In the process, of course, he interrogates Jim himself, who is at the same time conducting his own ongoing inquiry, one he hopes will end up vindicating him to himself. And there are, as we will see, other inquirers, other investigations.

But before Jim's self-interrogation begins, before Marlow's inquiry into Jim begins, and even before the magistrate's formal trial begins, there is another "inquiry" that deserves our attention: the lightning-quick, absurdly superficial exercise conducted in the lifeboat by three of the four officers who jumped. Beginning even before the sun has risen on an empty sea, it seeks to establish before anyone else can what happened, why the men did what they did, and why it was a perfectly justifiable thing that any rational person would have done.

This first "kangaroo court" procedure is one that Jim sits through in utter silence. That it is a sham designed to acquit all parties is suggested powerfully by Conrad's language, which conveys the breathless desperation of people trying to prove something to themselves, rather than trying to get at the bottom of things. The passage begins with one man testifying to an appreciative audience ready to corroborate his testimony. Before long Conrad simply drops all efforts at using quotation marks to show where one "witness" stops and another starts speaking:

> "I knew from the first she would go." "Not a minute too soon." "A narrow squeak, b'gosh!" . . . She was gone! She was gone! No doubt about it. Nobody could have helped. . . . Never doubted she would go. The lights were gone. No mistake. The lights were gone. Couldn't expect anything else. She had to go. . . . They concluded she would not have been long when she once started. It seemed to cause them some sort of satisfaction. They assured each other that she couldn't have been long about it—"Just shot down like a flat-iron." The chief engineer declared that the masthead light at the moment of sinking seemed to drop "like a lighted match you throw down." (115)

During the entire period in which the three officers who first abandoned ship are reaching their unanimous verdict about what happened, they believe that the fourth, silent member of their party is George, the acting third engineer who collapsed and died just before Jim jumped. When they find that it is Jim, not George, who shares their boat with them, they quickly conclude their inquiry into what happened and smugly place Jim on trial for nothing less—or more—than one man's murder.

This second, even more pernicious little inquiry is carried out mainly by the captain and chief engineer, who "yap before [Jim] like a couple of mean mongrels at a tree'd thief," as Jim recalls for Marlow: "Yap! yap! 'What are you doing here?' . . . Yap! yap! 'You ain't fit to live!' Yap! yap! Two of them trying to out-bark each other. . . . It was sweet to hear them; it kept me alive. . . . 'I wonder you had pluck enough to jump. You ain't wanted here. If I had known who it was, I would have tipped you over—you skunk. What have you done with the other? Where did you get the pluck to jump—you coward? What's to prevent us three from firing you overboard? . . . Murdering coward! . . . You killed him. You killed him'" (118–19). Before long, though, the captain and chief engineer decide to drop their trumped-up charges that Jim murdered their friend. Suddenly "they were friendly—oh! so damnably friendly!" Jim tells Marlow, "Chums, shipmates. All in the same boat. Make the best of it. They hadn't meant anything. They didn't care a hang for George. George had gone back to his berth for something at the last moment and got caught. The man was a manifest fool. Very sad, of course" (124). The other men have obviously come to realize that soon they will *all* be on trial, and for the murder of more than just one man. If they are to have a chance at convincing a judge of the results of their own facile inquiry into what happened, they will have to present a united and unanimous front.

Any chance of convincing anyone disappears, of course, when the story the men tell on being picked up by the *Avondale* is grossly contradicted by fact, for in reality—and despite all "evidence" to the contrary (the bulging bulkhead, the utter darkness of the sea soon after the jump)—the *Patna* never sank. That fact comes as unexpectedly as the floating derelict had earlier come in the night to check the seemingly unperturbable progress of the *Patna*. Indeed, the barely and inexplicably floating *Patna*, which had earlier been stopped in its "track" by the floating derelict, becomes, symbolically, the floating derelict that unexpectedly untracks the "story" the rescued officers tell. It proves them liars as well as officers who have been derelict in their duties. It virtually assures the judgment against them that the magistrate of the inquiry is eventually to hand down.

Thus, the magistrate's verdict—that the four should be stripped of their certificates—is something of an anticlimax, coming as it does in the novel's fourteenth chapter. For one thing, it has little effect on the future of several of the men. The captain doesn't even wait to hear the magistrate's disposition toward him; after testifying, he disappears. "Where?" Marlow asks his listeners rhetorically. "To Apia? to Honolulu? He had 6,000 miles of tropical belt to disport himself in. . . . He departed, disappeared, vanished, absconded. . . . The Pacific is indeed big; but whether he found a place for a display of his talents or not, the fact remains he had flown into a place like a witch on a broomstick" (47). As for the chief engineer, he is so deep in the throes of alcoholism that he suffers delirium tremens in a hospital before the case against him has even been made. The main punishment inflicted on the chief engineer is, in other words, the suffering he inflicts on himself with the bottle that has no doubt long been the source of his "courage."

Only Jim is significantly affected by the outcome of the formal inquiry, and even he can be said to be affected only in a superficial way. He figures that the lack of a certificate wouldn't prevent him from getting a job as a ship's "quartermaster" (80). And it certainly doesn't keep him from going to work for a man named Stein on an island remote from news of European-style inquiries and where, though he has no last name, he is given a new first one, Tuan, meaning "Lord." Jim suffers greatly, of course, from having participated in a lie and, even worse, from having jumped ship. But that suffering began long before any guilty verdict was handed down, as can be seen in the passage in which Jim, talking to Marlow, describes the other officers telling their collective story on being picked up by the *Avondale:* "'Shock slight. Stopped the ship. Ascertained the damage. Took measures to get the boats out without creating a panic. As the first boat was lowered ship went down in a squall. Sank like lead. . . . What could be more clear' . . . he hung his head . . . 'and more awful?' His lips quivered while he looked straight into my eyes. 'I had jumped—hadn't I?' he asked, dismayed. 'That's what I had to live down. The story didn't matter'" (133). The progress and outcome of the formal inquiry are in a sense preempted by this passage. What matters is that the men jumped, and that is a fact disputed by no one from the beginning. Nor can it be disputed, from the outcome of the inquiry, that the story the men gave on being picked up was false. Technically speaking, all the inquiry provides is an opportunity for testimony to become a matter of record and for a decision to be made as to the punishment to be inflicted.

In another sense, though, the inquiry provides something far more important. It causes people hearing the testimony to conduct inquiries of their own: inquiries into facts and reasons, to be sure, but also inquiries into their own moral natures and their beliefs about the moral fiber—or lack thereof—of human nature. In the remaining pages of this chapter, we will be focusing on three of Marlow's inquiries, those involving interviews with (a) the alcoholic chief engineer, (b) the French lieutenant who found the *Patna* floating and abandoned by its officers, and (c) Captain Brierly, one of the two assessors who participates in the formal proceedings. In focusing on Marlow's inquiry into Captain Brierly, we will implicitly and at the same time be focusing on an inquiry conducted by Brierly himself, outside the bounds of the formal inquiry in which he judges character in predictable, socially mandated ways. This last inquiry, by Brierly into Brierly, is as crucial to the novel as it is easy to overlook, for it advances the idea that our moral idealisms, our heroic accounts of human character, may be as paper-thin and rotten as the foredeck's bulkhead. It suggests that the beliefs we confidently offer in the light of day, in public spaces like churches and courtrooms, are as false and therefore vulnerable to fact as is the verbiage concocted by men who, "all in the same boat," concoct a story about coolheaded actions taken in the face of imminent danger.

The first of the characters in the *Patna* tragedy from whom Marlow attempts to learn something is the chief engineer. Marlow has gone to see an acquaintance of his own in the hospital the day before the inquiry is to begin. While he is there, quite by chance he sees "in the white men's ward that little chap tossing on his back, with his arm in splints, and quite light-headed" (48–49). This would be the second engineer, the little man who was himself drinking and speaking of "plates like brown paper" just as a sound like thunder rumbled up from deep in the hold. "To my great surprise," Marlow continues, the chief engineer "the long individual with the drooping white moustache, had also found his way there" (49). And why has the chief engineer been hospitalized? At Mariani's billiard room and "grog shop," Marlow has managed to hear, the chief engineer had been "keeping up his pecker with such tonics as Mariani dispensed . . . till the evening of the third day, when, after letting out a few horrible screams, he found himself compelled to seek safety in flight from a legion of centipedes. . . . The police plucked him off a garbage-heap early in the morning" (50). Now lying on a hospital bed, he is described by Marlow as looking like "a war-worn soldier with a child-like soul" but also with a "hint of spectral alarm that lurked in the blank glitter of his glance, resembling a nondescript form or terror crouching silently behind a pane of glass" (50).

Marlow takes an immediate interest in the chief engineer, in no small part because he has already seen and taken an immediate and sympathetic interest in Jim. Marlow says he knew from the first look he got at him that Jim was "the kind of fellow you would, on the strength of his looks, leave in charge of the deck—figuratively and professionally speaking. . . . I tell you I ought to know the right kind of looks. I would have trusted the deck to that youngster on the strength of a single glance" (44–45). If the chief engineer's "spectral alarm" has anything to do with Jim's case, if the "terror" causing him to "keep his pecker up" with gin has anything to do with fears Jim may be harboring, or if the nightmare visions of "legions of centipedes" have as their inspiration some horror Jim has experienced or is experiencing, then Marlow wants to know about them, for Marlow deeply identifies with Jim. Jim is Marlow's ideal image of himself; he is how Marlow pictures the person who has what we might call "the right stuff." He is, in Marlow's eyes, the epitome of humankind: attractive and moral at once, his morality legible in his very looks.

It may seem odd that Marlow would inquire into a man like Jim by first inquiring into the drunken psyche of the repulsive chief engineer, but it is at the same time appropriate. *Lord Jim* is a novel of indirection; it tells its story and analyzes its subject obliquely. If Conrad tells his tale indirectly, at several levels of remove from his audience, by having a narrator who has been Marlow's most interested listener tell us a story related by Marlow, then is it not appropriate that Marlow himself be the one who makes these oblique inquiries and seeks to come to know Jim *indirectly?* Indirection is, after all, our own manner of inquiry into this text, the way that, as readers, *we* come to know Jim.

The inquiry into Jim as a character and an ideal via an interrogation of someone barely tangential to him even makes sense in light of the cosmic vision, or metaphysics, of *Lord Jim*. If the great mysteries are "Unknowable" in Conrad's view, then—again, in Conrad's view—it may make more sense to approach them by stepping away from them than to interrogate them directly. Indirection may be the only direction toward knowledge of those things which fascinate or elude us, be they the God that Jim's father foolishly pretends knowledge of or the "Lord" that Jim's father's son eventually is to become.

Marlow, who in *Lord Jim* as in *Heart of Darkness* serves as Conrad's Everyman, explains in perhaps less complex—but by no means simple—terms why he sought knowledge of Jim by approaching the alcoholic engineer. "He was so extremely calm," Marlow begins by saying, "that I began to indulge in the eccentric hope of hearing something explanatory of the famous affair from his point of view. You may call it an unhealthy curiosity if you like; but I have a distinct notion I wished to find something, some profound and redeeming cause, some merciful explanation, some convincing shadow of an excuse. I see well enough now that I hoped for the impossible—for the laying of what is the most obstinate ghost of man's creation, of the uneasy doubt uprising like a mist, secret and gnawing like a worm, and more chilling than the certitude of death." That "most obstinate ghost" and "uneasy doubt" is, Marlow says, "the doubt of the sovereign power enthroned in a fixed standard of conduct" (50).

If Marlow cannot maintain faith in Jim, then he cannot retain faith either in himself or in the possibility of human beings living up to a high, noble, and ennobling code. And the desire to maintain those faiths is what fuels his personal inquiry. "Did I believe in a miracle?"

Marlow asks his listeners. "And why did I desire it so ardently? Was it for my own sake that I wished to find some shadow of an excuse . . . ? I was, and make no mistake, looking for a miracle." The miracle Marlow is here referring to is, incredible as it may seem, evidence from the mouth of the chief engineer of the viability of fixed standards of conduct: "I positively hoped to obtain from that battered and shady invalid some exorcism against the ghost of a doubt" (51).

The response Marlow obtains to his question about the *Patna* is hardly the one he is looking—and hoping—for. The chief engineer "repeated *Patna?* interrogatively, seemed to make a short effort of memory and said: 'Quite right. I am an old stager out here. I saw her go down.'" Marlow isn't about to accept what he already knows to be "a stupid lie"; he is nearly ready to "vent" his "indignation" when his interlocutor adds, "She was full of reptiles" (51). Marlow is so taken aback by the explanation that his desire to indignantly refute it is checked. "What did he mean?" Marlow asked himself, as "the unsteady phantom of terror behind [the engineer's] glassy eye seemed to look into [Marlow's] wistfully." Marlow seems to be ready to give the subject of his inquiry the benefit of the doubt by assuming that he means the *Patna* was figuratively or symbolically full of reptiles. But the chief engineer seems to think he means what he said, literally, for he tries to ground it in visual evidence. "Suddenly my interesting invalid," Marlow says, "shot out an arm thick like a tentacle and clawed my shoulder. The chief engineer continues: "only my eyes were good enough to see. I am famous for my eyesight. . . . I tell you there are no such eyes as mine this side of the Persian Gulf. Look under the bed" (52).

As if on command, Marlow "stoop[s] instantly." When he does, the chief engineer asks, "What do you see?" When Marlow says "Nothing," he is answered by the claim that "if I were to look I could see—there's no eyes like mine, I tell you." At that point, the chief engineer proves his supposedly greater sight by looking under the bed himself and pronouncing, "Millions of pink toads. There's no eyes like mine. Millions of pink toads. It's worse than seeing a ship sink" (52).

Marlow is arrested by the experience—or he is, rather, until a voice hails him from a distance, warning him not to "let [the chief engineer] start hollering." But that warning serves only to heighten the chief engineer's intensity. "The ship was full of them, you know," he continues, while "leer[ing] . . . knowingly." And "'We had to clear out on the strict Q.T.,' he whispered with extreme rapidity. 'All pink. All pink—as big as mastiffs, with an eye on the top of the head and claws all round their ugly mouths'" (53). Suddenly he thinks again, not of the toads that were back on the *Patna* but, rather, of those he believes to be under his bed. "'Ssh! what are they doing now down there?' he asked, pointing to the floor with fantastic precautions of voice and gesture. . . . 'They are all awake—millions of them. They are trampling on me! . . . Help! H-e-elp!'" (54).

Marlow confesses to have been "fairly routed" from the hospital by what he has heard. Still, he says, "the howl pursued me like a vengeance" all the way to his residence, where he runs into a surgeon involved with the inquiry. The surgeon comments that although "the head" of the chief engineer is "all gone," the "curious part is there's some sort of method in his ravings. I am trying to find out." The surgeon continues by treating what the alcoholic invalid says in the manner of a Freudian psychoanalyst. "Traditionally he ought to see snakes," the doctor comments to Marlow, "but he doesn't." When Marlow cuts the conversation short by "assuming an air of regret," "shak[ing] hands in a hurry," and walking off, the surgeon "cries after" him: "I say, . . . he can't attend that inquiry. Is his evidence material?" (55).

The answer that Marlow calls back—"Not in the least"—has to be considered carefully. For one thing, by saying that the chief engineer can provide no "material" evidence, Marlow is not exactly saying that what he has heard from the chief engineer has been worthless as far as his own inquiry is concerned. Is not Marlow himself looking for "some convincing *shadow* of an excuse" with which to lay the "*ghost* of man's creation," namely, an "uneasy doubt uprising like a mist" (emphasis added)? Perhaps the chief engineer's admittedly *im*material visions can help shadow forth some part of the truth Marlow so assiduously seeks.

For another thing, even if we were to interpret Marlow's assertion as meaning that the chief engineer is little more than a madman, we would have to recognize that such madness might be of interest to Marlow. What has caused him to drink himself into alcoholic insanity? Given that there were no more pink toads crawling around in the hold of the *Patna* than there are now pink toads crawling around under a hospital bed, the question arises: What *did* the man experience that he now still sees, perhaps mercifully disguised psychologically in the form of pink toads? Something has caused the sanity of this man, who now speaks incessantly of his superior sight, to "flake," as surely as the pressure of the water has caused the bulkhead plate to pop. Did he see Evil incarnate just before he jumped, the same Evil whose temptations caused the Fall of humankind from the Garden of Eden? The notion may seem highly speculative, but it is one of many possibilities, some of them irreconcilable, that the text may quietly be suggesting. "Traditionally, he ought to see snakes" has been the surgeon's odd suggestion. Is it not possible that the chief engineer has had that "keen perception" of what the narrator, in the novel's opening pages, calls "the Intolerable"—that which our culture figures by the serpent and which is pictured in the mind of the chief engineer in the form of pink toads?

If "the Intolerable" is what the chief engineer has seen, if that is the source of his now-immaterial visions, then Marlow has learned something important, something that would be reason for allaying doubt and maintaining belief in Jim, in himself, in his culture's faith in moral standards, and in humankind. After all, the "perception" of "the Intolerable," though it has driven Jim "away for good from seaports and white men, even into the virgin forests" of Malaysia, has not destroyed his sanity or his desire to do good. If some human beings can survive what others cannot, then there is reason to believe in the possibility of difference, in the possibility that although some people are little better than beasts, others—if not a little less than Gods—are a little better than, and therefore lords among, men. That possibility is, after all, what the Western conception of and faith in heroism rests on.

After the Fall: The Inquiries

The next of the three characters Marlow interrogates as part of his inquiry into Jim, himself, and his own cultural ideal would also suggest that human difference is possible, and therefore that there is reason to believe some will succeed and do good when others succumb to the temptation to do evil. This second man is one of the French officers who boarded the *Patna* shortly after finding it thronged with passengers, abandoned by its officers, and "floating dangerously by the head" (137).

Marlow interviews the elderly officer in a Sydney café, years after the formal inquiry into the *Patna* affair has been concluded. The Frenchman, who is by then serving as third lieutenant on the *Victorieuse,* recalls boarding the derelict steamer, being pressed by a "mob" of "agitate[d]" pilgrims, seeing the corpse of the white sailor on deck, and then examining the bulkhead, which he says he advised the commander to "leave alone, it was so villainous to look at" (139). Next, he remembers, they got "two hawsers on board . . . and took the *Patna* in tow," hoping against hope that its bulkhead would not give way en route to "the nearest English port." Hardly confident that it would remain afloat while being pulled through resisting seas, the French commander stationed "two quartermasters . . . with axes by the hawsers, to cut us clear of our tow in case she . . ." Here the French lieutenant "fluttered downwards his heavy eyelids, making his meaning as plain as possible. . . . 'What would you! One does what one can (*on fait ce qu'on peut*)'" (140).

Marlow, who doubtless assumes the lieutenant is being a bit defensive here about actions that might be seen as overly careful or even cowardly, can hardly have expected what he next hears. The French lieutenant "clasped his hands on his stomach again. 'I remained on board that—that—my memory is going *(s'en va). Ah! Patt-nà. C'est bien ça. Patt-nà. Merci.* It is droll how one forgets. I stayed on that ship thirty hours.'" When Marlow exclaims his surprise, the French lieutenant "pursed his lips a little. . . . 'It was judged proper,' he said, lifting his eyebrows dispassionately, that one of the officers should remain to keep an eye open (*pour ouvrir l'oeil*)' . . . he sighed idly . . . 'and for communicating by signals with the towing ship—do you see?—and so on. For the rest, it was my opinion too. We made our boats ready to drop over—and I also on that ship took measures. . . . *Enfin!* One has done one's possible. It was a delicate position. Thirty hours'" (141). In the old French lieutenant, Marlow meets a man who has lived up to a fixed code of conduct by doing what is "judged proper," whatever the risk. Not that he stayed on the *Patna* with pilgrims only because others decided that someone should remain with them; "it was my opinion to [remain]" as well, he tells Marlow.

To have wanted to act, and to have acted, in a way that is at once selfless, dangerous, and "judged proper" by others is, of course, to have acted heroically, although the French lieutenant has a way of describing heroic action in such a modest and uninflated way as to make it sound perfectly ordinary. But that modesty, as reflected in matter-of-fact language, is important. Finally, the kind of heroism that would justify our faith in the viability of idealistic codes of conduct may simply involve doing what it *seems* like anyone would do because, after all, it is the only proper thing *to* do. The language of the hero would thus inevitably be simple and straightforward. It would probably be unmarked by poetic or epic diction of the kind that, as a young man, Jim encountered in romantic books, precisely because the hero would be unconscious of the fact that his actions were extraordinary.

The French lieutenant's language, in its directness and simplicity, recalls the language of the "below-decks hero" of the training vessel—the boy who fished a drowning man out of a gale-swept sea at great risk to himself. ("I just saw his head bobbing, and I dashed my boat-hook into the water. It caught in his breeches and I nearly went overboard, . . . only Old Symons let go the tiller and grabbed my legs—the boat nearly swamped. Old Symons is a fine chap.") Of course, the old Frenchman's language, unlike that of the young Englishman saved by Old Symons, is at times somewhat difficult to follow, because it is not the speaker's original tongue. ("One has done one's possible," the Frenchman remarks.) At some points, the lieutenant seems to be resorting to his native French, and at other points it seems that the English we are reading is Marlow's rough translation of something that has been said in French. Then again, the language of the lower-decks hero was at least as difficult, if not more so, for Jim to interpret than the lieutenant's French proves difficult for Marlow. If it hadn't been, Jim wouldn't have misread it as "a pitiful display of vanity."

What I am suggesting is this: that the lieutenant's simple, straightforward style is at once (a) foreign and (b) foregrounded *as* foreign by the sprinkling of italicized French words may itself be significant. Symbolically, the foreignness of the hero's simple language and the fact that, even when translated, it can sound a bit rough and odd, only reinforces that the hero is *different,* not "one of us," as Marlow several times calls Jim. The hero's unassuming simplicity needs translating by those of us who cannot imagine that is not vanity of a perverse form, and who certainly cannot imagine remaining for 30 hours on board a boat that may suddenly sink in an inescapable vortex. Simple though it may be, the language of heroes is a language of difference, precisely because it is a language of *differents.*

The French lieutenant, then—the second of the three men whose character Marlow interrogates as part of his inquiry into Jim, himself, and his own cultural ideal—would seem generally to suggest the same thing the chief engineer had earlier. That is, it is possible for Marlow to conclude from his examination of the French lieutenant the same thing he is able to conclude from his bizarre encounter with the man envisioning immaterial toads. Human difference, Marlow is free to conclude, is indeed possible; therefore, the faith that some people will succeed and do good when all others would fail and succumb to the temptation to do evil is tenable, even desirable. Here, though, all similarity between the two episodes must be seen to end. The encounter with the chief engineer makes it possible to infer that Jim is one of those capable of looking into the abyss and surviving it while others collapse. The interview with the French lieutenant would suggest that Jim is *not* what I have called "a different." He is but one who flinches when almost all other people flinch. The French lieutenant, the text tells us, left Marlow "alone and discouraged—discouraged about Jim's case" (149).

Marlow at first refuses to accept the Frenchman's verdict. But the old lieutenant simply will not let him. "'And so that poor young man ran away along with the others,' he said, with grave tranquillity. . . . '*S'est enfui avec les autres*'" (145). Marlow, though he secretly admires "the discrimination of the man," his ability to "get hold of the only thing I cared about," nonetheless resists the equation of Jim with cowardice. But the French lieutenant again counters that resistance, not with an attack on the character of a young man who ran but, rather, with the humble assertion that *all* people are born cowards. Noble behavior, he argues, must be learned: "It would be too easy otherwise. But habit—habit—necessity—do you see?—the eye of others—*voilà*. . . . [O]ne's courage does not come of itself *(ne vient pas tout seul)*. There's nothing much in that to get upset about. One truth the more ought not to make life impossible. . . . But honour—the honour, monsieur! . . . The honour . . . that is real—that is!" (147–48).

The same belief in honor, in the fact that officers can and should simply develop bravery as a habit, seems to be represented by Captain Brierly, another of the men Marlow interrogates in the process of inquiring into himself, his ideal self-projection (Jim), and the viability of codes of conduct in those moments when human beings need them most. It is because Brierly has been judged a man of difference, a ship's captain who, like the French lieutenant, has always managed to live up to what is "judged proper," that he has been chosen to serve as one of the two assessors under the magistrate conducting the formal inquiry into the *Patna* affair.

We are introduced to Brierly as Marlow introduces him to an audience of listeners: "One of the assessors was a sailing-ship skipper with a reddish beard, and of a pious disposition. Brierly was the other. Big Brierly. Some of you must have heard of Big Brierly—the captain of the crack ship of the Blue Star line. That's the man."

The three-word sentence "That's the man," perhaps because of its very brevity, has a definitive quality to it. It is as if Brierly epitomizes man, as if he is *the* man personified. The sentences following would seem to justify such an interpretation: "He seemed consumedly bored by the honour thrust upon him. He had never in his life made a mistake, never had an accident, never a mishap, never a check in his steady rise, and he seemed to be one of those lucky fellows who know nothing of indecision, much less of self-mistrust. He had saved lives at sea, had rescued ships in distress, had a gold chronometer presented to him by the underwriters, and a pair of binoculars with a suitable inscription from some foreign Government, in commemoration of these services" (57). He has not only the look of a leader but the tickets and badges that certify he is the real thing. He is, to be sure, "acutely aware of his merits" ("in his opinion there was not such another commander"), but his lack of humility does not seem to be equatable with that pride which goes before a tragic fall (57). "As I looked at him flanking on one side the unassuming pale-faced magistrate who presided at the inquiry," Marlow recalls, "his self-satisfaction presented to me and the world a surface as hard as granite" (57–58).

Brierly is, publicly at least, highly critical of the officers who abandoned the *Patna,* Jim included. With embarrassing simplicity he explains to the court why these men saw no lights when they looked toward where the *Patna* had been from the vantage point of their lifeboat. It is partly on his advice, of course, that the magistrate decides to strip Jim of his certificate.

Even privately, Brierly can be scathingly critical. "This is a disgrace," he says at one point to Marlow, who has sought out his conversation much in the way he has sought out the chief engineer's, much as he will later seek out the French lieutenant's.

> We've got all kinds amongst us—some anointed scoundrels in the lot; but, hang it, we must preserve professional decency or we become no better than so many tinkers going about loose. We are trusted. Do you understand?—trusted! Frankly, I don't care a snap for all the pilgrims that ever came out of Asia, but a decent man would not have behaved like this to a full cargo of old rags in bales. We aren't an organized body of men, and the only thing that holds us together is just the name for that kind of decency. Such an affair destroys one's confidence. (68)

The speech is as powerful an expression as there is in the novel of faith in the possibility of difference, of the fact that since it takes "all kinds" to make a world, there are high heroes and low scoundrels, some "decent" human beings among "so many tinkers."

But at other times, in private, Brierly's "thoughts" take another "direction," a direction that causes Marlow to "wonder . . . greatly" (66). At these dark times, Brierly makes Marlow wonder if the "confidence" the *Patna* incident has destroyed is Brierly's confidence in himself and, beyond that, in the possibility of human beings so decent that no situation could make them cower or act like scoundrels. Brierly, like Marlow, it seems, is attracted to and sees himself in Jim. "Why are we tormenting that young chap?" he asks Marlow at one point. He also wants to know why Jim doesn't just flee the inquiry, as his captain has done. "'Nothing can save him. He's done for.' We walked on in silence a few steps. 'Why eat all that dirt?'" (66). When Marlow explains that, for one thing, "It costs some money to run away," Brierly stuns him by showing a willingness to pay for the escape of one who has helped destroy his confidence. "I tell you what," Brierly responds. "I will put up two hundred rupees if you put up another hundred and undertake to make the beggar clear out early tomorrow morning" (67).

In the word *beggar* Brierly may seem to be preserving a sense of his own difference. But that sense of difference seems also to be erased when, "very soon after" the inquiry, he "committed suicide" (58): "He jumped overboard at sea barely a week after the end of the Inquiry, and less than three days after leaving port on his outward passage; as though in that exact spot in the midst of waters he had suddenly perceived the gates of the other world flung open wide for his reception. Yet it was not a sudden impulse" (59). Brierly, while talking a hard line, has evidently been conducting a quiet, internal inquiry. His verdict has turned out to be guilty; he has consequently sentenced himself to death.

Marlow later interviews a man named Jones who became captain of the *Ossa* on the day Brierly fell by jumping. "'Why did he commit the rash act, Captain Marlow—can you think?' asked Jones, pressing his palms together." Marlow replies, "You may depend on it, Captain Jones. [I]t wasn't anything that would have disturbed much either of us two . . . [N]either you nor I, sir, had ever thought so much of ourselves" (65).

To an extent, of course, Marlow's statement is true, and Brierly's fall is just another example of the inevitable end of pride. But in another sense, Marlow is dissembling, disturbed as he is by the very thing Brierly must have been disturbed by. For Marlow, as for Brierly, Jim's jump from the *Patna,* his fall from grace, as it were, has the power to eradicate the possibility of "self-satisfaction hard as granite," of a firm faith in the nobility of the human race.

6

After the Inquiries: The Quest

Before Captain Brierly's suicide, and even before the inquiry is over, Marlow asks Jim what he will do if and when a judgment goes against him. Jim does not take the question lightly: "he would not know where to turn, he confessed, clearly thinking aloud rather than talking to me. Certificate gone, career broken, no money to get away, no work that he could obtain as far as I could see." What Jim seems to dread is not the disapproval of others but, rather, the simple fact that, if found guilty, he will have lost his career, his living, his earning potential. "Apparently," Marlow concludes, "he held Brierly's contemptuous opinion of these proceedings ordained by law" (80).

Because Jim seems as outwardly contemptuous of the legal proceedings as the assessor is privately, Marlow tries to get him to flee before the trial is concluded—as Brierly privately believes he should. "There was no morality in the impulse which induced me to lay before him Brierly's plan of evasion," Marlow says, recalling a dinner he had with Jim just before the verdict was due. "There were all the rupees—absolutely ready in my pocket and very much at his service. Oh! a loan; a loan of course—and if an introduction to a man (in Rangoon) who could put some work in his way . . . Why! with the greatest pleasure" (152).

Contemptuous though he seems to be of the legal proceedings and worried solely (as it would appear he is) about his prospects of finding a job and making money, Jim nonetheless shocks Marlow by immediately rejecting Brierly's behind-the-scenes offer. As Marlow expresses it, with uncharacteristic succinctness, "the subtle intentions of my immorality were defeated by the moral simplicity of the criminal." For some reason, it seems, Jim "was eager to go through the ceremony of execution. . . . 'Clear out! Couldn't think of it,' he said, with a shake of the head" (153). Marlow is at first "angry" about, as well as surprised by, Jim's quick rejection of Brierly's curious but generous offer.

> "The whole wretched business," I said, "is bitter enough, I should think, for a man of your kind. . . ."
>
> "You don't seem to understand," he said, incisively; then looking at me without a wink, "I may have jumped, but I don't run away." (153–54)

We cannot be sure precisely why Jim rejects the loan of rupees and the introduction to the man in Rangoon, but we cannot go too far wrong in guessing that he does so out of a recuperated belief that circumstances have created false evidence about his true character. To accept money from an assessor and fail to remain to hear his verdict would, in Jim's view, be tantamount to admitting to his judges, the world, and himself that he has no remaining faith in himself, no remaining doubt about the significance of what happened. To take Brierly's money and run would be to confirm that he has little more pride than a common beggar. And, miraculous though it may seem, Jim is not utterly devoid of pride. That he isn't can be seen in the fact that, worried as he is about the prospects of unemployment, he will not go home to England. "At home," he has confided to Marlow, he "could perhaps get something; but it meant going to his people for help, and that he would not do" (80).

Marlow apparently learns something from Jim's rejection, both of the rupees and of the chance of being introduced to Brierly's contact in Rangoon. Later, he hears the magistrate pronounce Jim guilty of "utter disregard of . . . plain duty" and of "abandoning in the moment of danger the lives and property confided in [his] charge." Just after that, Marlow meets an Australian named Chester, who figures Jim may be just the man to fill an unattractive but open position—a position no decent, self-respecting person would want. But Marlow has read in the rejection of Brierly's offer a persistent or renewed unwillingness, on Jim's part, to believe in his own unworthiness. And so he balks at serving as Chester's go-between.

Chester, a "pearler, wrecker, trader, whaler," and "anything and everything a man may be at sea, but a pirate," has recently "discovered . . . a guano island somewhere" that is dangerous to approach and even more perilous to anchor in. Nonetheless, the place is, as he puts it to Marlow, "As good as a gold-mine"—so lucrative, in fact, that in light of the refusal by any number of ship's captains to help him export guano to civilization, Chester has made up his mind to buy his own steamer and risk wrecking it in order to "cart the blessed stuff [him]self" (161). But he needs someone willing to live on a mountain of bird excrement, where "There are whole years when not a drop of rain falls," and oversee the mining operation (167).

Chester figures he has found his man in Jim. "I want that young chap," he tells Marlow, to which Marlow responds by saying, "I don't understand." The narrative continues: "'He's no good, is he?' said Chester, crisply. 'I know nothing about it,' I protested. 'Why, you told me yourself he was taking it to heart,' argued Chester. 'Well, in my opinion a chap who . . . Anyhow, he can't be much good; but then you see I am on the look-out for someone on my island.' He nodded significantly. 'I'm going to dump forty coolies there—if I've got to steal 'em. Somebody must work the stuff. . . . Let him take charge. Make him supreme boss over the coolies'" (166–67). Chester has already learned the value in taking on those who have been made to feel like social pariahs. His subservient "partner" is a man known as Old Robinson, a man who, like Jim, would seem to have a past too unseemly to live down. "Holy-Terror" Robinson, as he is also sometimes called, was once shipwrecked with six other men on "the west side of Stewart Island" but was found alone, sometime later, "kneeling on the kelp, naked as the day he was born, and chanting some psalm tune or other." To clarify what he is implying, Chester put[s] his lips to Marlow's ear. "Cannibal?" he asks suggestively. "[W]ell, they used to give him the name years and years ago" (162).

But Marlow cannot see Jim living on a guano island. Nor can he see Jim seeing himself there. "Holy Terror" Robinson may have accepted society's definition of him as subhuman, but Jim, in his pride, still—or, at least, once again—thinks of himself as not only human but good, not only good but noble. And so, in response to Chester, Marlow at first says nothing, but instead has "a rapid vision of Jim perched on a shadowless rock, up to his knees in guano, with the screams of sea-birds in his ears, the incandescent ball of the sun above his head; the empty sky and the empty ocean all a-quiver, simmering together in the heat as far as the eye could reach." Finally, he responds verbally to Chester: "'I wouldn't advise my worst enemy . . .' I began. 'What's the matter with you?' cried Chester; 'I mean to give him . . . two six-shooters in his belt. . . . Surely he wouldn't be afraid of anything forty coolies could do—with two six-shooters and he the only armed man too!'" (167).

Chester clearly conceives of Jim not only as a pariah but as a coward as well. One last time he asks if Marlow won't recommend that Jim take control of 40 coolies and guano island. "Certainly not," Marlow answers; "moreover, I am sure he wouldn't. He is badly cut up, but he isn't mad as far as I know." Chester responds indignantly: "He is no earthly good for anything. . . . If you only could see a thing as it is, you would see it's the very thing for him" (167). Marlow, who sometimes fears that he doesn't see Jim as he is, later tries to see things Chester's way, and he almost writes Jim a letter describing, and recommending that Jim seriously consider, Chester's offer. Finally, though, he cannot. "He was—" Marlow later tells an audience listening to Jim's story, "if you will allow me to say so—very fine; very fine—and very unfortunate" (177).

In chapter 1 of this study, we saw Jim's pride in thinking of himself as being as far above other boys as the foretop of his training vessel was above the deck. We saw how that pride preceded Jim's tragic fall, and why it may have even contributed to it. Pride kept Jim from truly knowing himself, from coming to a realistic assessment of his own strengths and weaknesses. The lack of self-knowledge, in turn, allowed him to sail the oceans oblivious to and therefore unprepared for those unexpected shocks and challenges which are always possible.

Once Jim's fall from the *Patna* has occurred, though, a curious thing happens: we begin to view Jim's pride differently. Suddenly, it seems not so much the cause of his fall from nobility as it seems curiously, even absurdly, ennobling. Jim has, after all, only three choices to make following his leap from the *Patna* and the subsequent inquiry into his behavior. The choice he makes helps us to feel that, as Marlow says, he is "very fine" as well as "very unfortunate."

Jim could, after all, have simply accepted as truth the notion of his utter unworthiness, the view—as Chester puts it—that he is "no earthly good for anything." Alongside Old Robinson, a man who has apparently learned to live with a very debased and ugly self-definition, he could devote the rest of his years to living in a place—and trading in a commodity—reflective of society's view of his worth. Or, conversely, he could have accepted as true the notion of his unworthiness but shown an unwillingness to live with that truth. He could easily, in other words, have taken the route taken by Captain Brierly, who presumably committed suicide on confronting the fact of his unworthiness.

But there would have been nothing ennobling about becoming a guano exporter, and, as for suicide, it smacks as much of cowardice as of disappointed idealism. Brierly's death, after all, posed a pointed question even as it afforded an instructive parallel: if it is cowardly to jump from a ship in trouble, is it not equally cowardly to bail out of life, just because you come face to face with the fact that you, too, *might* bail out of a ship in trouble?

Instead, Jim does the only other thing he could have done: he refuses to accept the judgment that he is unworthy. In rejecting as false that verdict on his character passed first by circumstance and later in court, Jim chooses to seek a new start, a new place, and a new set of circumstances in which he can establish the *truth* of his bright old self-image rather than accepting its falsehood, as Brierly has done, or accepting a dark new alternative, as people like Chester would have him do. Proud as ever, Jim nonetheless earns our sympathies by insisting on living as if he is worthy of trust and respect while waiting for opportunities to prove himself worthy of both.

And so Marlow, rather than relating Chester's offer, waits and instead gives Jim a letter of introduction to a friend. He persuades Jim to accept his help by getting him to "look at the letter" and see that he has written it "in terms that one only ventures to use when speaking of an intimate friend," thus making clear that he is not asking someone to do or repay him a favor. "I make myself unreservedly responsible for you," Marlow then adds, thereby revealing something even more important, namely, that he *believes* in Jim, believes that Jim is justified in believing in himself, and believes that Jim will someday succeed in his quest to establish the validity of his faith in himself.

Jim's response to Marlow's faithful gesture is significant: "'Jove!' he gasped out. 'It is noble of you'" (183). Nobility, clearly, is something Jim still believes in. He sees it in Marlow's willingness to see it in him. Furthermore, he sees evidence, in a noble man's faith in himself, that his own persisting dream of a noble identity is not entirely unfounded. "You *have* helped me," he blurts out. ". . . You have given me confidence . . . yes . . . clean slate" (184–85). Saying that he "must go now," Jim initiates a quest the goal or end of which is to utterly refute the verdict of the inquest.

For a while, it seems, Jim's quest will prove to be relatively short and easy. "Six months afterwards," Marlow tells his audience, "my friend . . . wrote to me, and judging, from the warmth of my recommendation, that I would like to hear, enlarged a little upon Jim's perfections. . . . Jim . . . was blooming" (187). Before long, however, Marlow returns from a trip to find two more letters awaiting his attention. The first, from the friend with whom Jim has been living and for whom he has been working in a rice mill, begins with the line "There are no spoons missing, as far as I know." The second letter, from Jim himself, explains why he left his host like a thief in the night: "That little second engineer of the *Patna* . . . turned up in a more or less destitute state, and got a temporary job of looking after the machinery of the mill." Jim says he couldn't "stand the familiarity of the little beast. . . . I am now for the time with Egstrom & Blake, ship-chandlers" (189).

That position, too, proves to be a false end of Jim's quest for respectability and self-respect. Another small reminder of the great, unexpected event of his past once again turns up almost like a piece of flotsam from what is left of a floating derelict. This time, it isn't the second engineer that floats in with the tide but, rather, "a steamer with returning pilgrims from the Red Sea." Some of them "were talking about it," Jim tells Marlow; still worse, Jim overhears a captain, upon learning about the *Patna* incident, say: "It's a disgrace to human natur'—that's what it is. I would despise being seen in the same room with one of those men. Yes sir!" (193–94). Jim's quest for renewed faith in his old, heroic self-conception cannot be realized among men who have predetermined that he is a disgrace to nature.

Jim next finds employment in Bangkok, working for Ucker Brothers, charterers and teak merchants. Marlow arrives there just in time to learn that Jim has been held responsible for a violent outbreak in Schomberg's tavern. A lieutenant in the Royal Siamese Navy, it seems, has made "some scornful remark" at Jim's expense; Jim, perhaps incorrectly assuming that the remark referred to his part in the *Patna* incident, has thrown the lieutenant into the harbor. Marlow later comments that, as a result of this, "the worst incident of all in his—his retreat. . . . I took him away from Bangkok in my ship, and we had a longish passage" (200).

In the word *retreat* Marlow seems to show consciousness that Jim's quest *for* a noble identity is so far only a form of running *from* an allegedly ignoble one. It is, Marlow seems to realize, bound to remain that way, too, as long as Jim is living and working where bits and pieces of knowledge about his past can turn up. Perhaps Marlow's awareness of Jim's plight and need for change is what leads him to take Jim "away from Bangkok" on "a *longish* passage" to work selling ship's stores for a man named De Jongh; perhaps it is what, soon after, prompts him to ask Jim, "Would you like . . . to leave this part of the world altogether; try California or the West Coast?" (200–1; emphasis added). Jim will never be what he wants to be, and believes he is, by running utterly away from civilization—to a desolate guano island, for instance—but he may have to establish citizenship in a truly new and different world of men and women.

In the end, it isn't the American New World where Marlow helps Jim initiate a quest that is not simultaneously a retreat, but it is *a* new world—indeed, it is, if anything, an even more remote Paradise. And it is a rare individual known to Marlow—"a wealthy and respected merchant" named Stein, in control of "a large inter-island [trading] business"—who helps Marlow help Jim find that new world, that apparently "clean slate" where he can attempt to rewrite for himself the identity he once found reflected in his reading.

Stein, though a minor character, is in many ways the most important and controversial character in *Lord Jim*. What he says about life, and about Jim, has been much debated by critics, who nonetheless agree on one thing: whether we read Conrad's novel optimistically or pessimistically, how we assess Conrad's broader worldview depends largely on how we interpret what Stein tells Marlow when Marlow comes "anxious to seek his advice" (202).

Stein, Marlow tells us, "possessed an intrepidity of spirit and a physical courage that could have been called reckless had it not been like a natural function of the body—say good digestion, for instance—completely unconscious of itself" (203). Born in Bavaria, Stein had taken "an active part" in "the revolutionary movement of 1848," eventually having to "make [an] escape" and take refuge "with a poor republican watchmaker in Trieste. From there he made his way, hawking watches, all the way to Tripoli, where a famous Dutch naturalist met him and, "engaging him as a sort of assistant," took him to the East. After four or more years of collecting insects and birds, the great naturalist went home, "and Stein, having no home to go to, remained with an old trader" he had befriended (205).

The trader, an old Scotsman who had formed a "privileged friendship" with the queen of the Wajo States in the Celebes, had until Stein's arrival been "the only white man allowed to reside in the country at that time" (205). Once Stein, though, had been declared "my son" by the dying Scotsman, he inherited not only the older man's "privileged position" but also "all his stock-in-trade, together with a fortified house on the banks of the only navigable river in the country" (206). On the old queen's death, Stein and one of her younger sons "became the heroes of innumerable exploits" during years in which "the country became disturbed by various pretenders to the throne."

Although the young heir, Mohammed Bonso, was eventually "assassinated at the gate of his own royal residence . . . on his return from a successful deer hunt"—and although Stein subsequently left that country for more peaceful islands and a more solitary life—it was not before he and Mohammed Bonso had had "wonderful adventures, and once stood a siege in the Scotsman's house for a month, with only a score of followers against a whole army. . . . I believe the natives," Marlow impresses on his listeners, "talk of that war to this day. Meantime, it seems, Stein never failed to annex on his own account every butterfly or beetle he could lay hands on" (206).

Famous as he still is among natives of the Celebes Wajo States for his "innumerable" heroic "exploits" and "adventures," Stein is still better known in Europe for the natural specimens he managed to "annex" between "negotiations, false truces, sudden outbreaks, reconciliation, treachery, and so on" (206)—and before his friend, "poor Mohammed Bonso," was assassinated: "His collection of *Buprestidoe* and *Longicorns*—beetles all—horrible miniature monsters, looking malevolent in death and immobility, and his cabinet of butterflies, beautiful and hovering under the glass of cases on lifeless wings, had spread his fame far over the earth. The name of this merchant, adventurer, sometime adviser of a Malay sultan . . . had, on account of a few bushels of dead insects, become known to learned persons in Europe, who could have had no conception, and certainly would not have cared to know anything, of his life or character. I, who knew," Marlow says, "considered him an eminently suitable person to receive my confidences about Jim's difficulties" (203).

Critics have disagreed about what the butterfly and the beetle (some would say the butterfly versus the beetle) collections suggest about Stein and his character. Questions such as the following have been implicitly and explicitly asked. Do they show something other than what is suggested by the heroic deeds done during the same period? Do they, in other words, undercut the view of Stein as a man of "reckless," almost "unconscious" action? Do they show him to be a possessive, imperialist "annexer" and thus very different from the idealistic revolutionary he has seemed to be? Do they, together or in contrast to one another, reveal contradictions in his identity or character? And the questions have been answered at length, often in ways as contrasting and contradictory as beetles and butterflies, fighting and collecting.

It seems fair enough to assume, though, that Stein's interest in butterflies can be read as an interest in beauty, and that his interest in catching, killing, and mounting such creatures suggests a desire to catch and fix beauty before it fades, passes, or changes to something else (perhaps even into an ugly beetle). If we make that assumption, we might also decide to assume that there is a connection between Stein's interest in butterflies and his life, first as a democratic revolutionary and later as a young prince's heroic ally against whole armies of antagonistic pretenders. Stein is, perhaps, to use a word he later uses, a "romantic," a believer in beautiful ideas, ideals, and forms, however frail and fleeting they may be. His impossible dream—*his* quest, the motive behind *his* global travels—is to make them permanent, and he lives by the dream even though he also knows that they are vulnerable and frail, prone to die, fall, and fail.

The collection of beetles—as squat, "horrible," and darkly monstrous as the butterflies are "beautiful," light, and "hovering"—can be seen as magnifying that ugly fact of existence which the narrator has earlier called "the Intolerable." They represent a reality the inevitable triumph of which Stein knows about all too well, thanks to the crushing defeat first of his revolutionary movement and later of his friend, "poor Mohammed Bonso," the son of the Wajo queen. If he ever could have, Stein can no longer deny the existence of what the "malevolent" beetles represent. Thus, to be honest about the nature of nature, about the harsh fact that is the earthly condition we find ourselves in, he must collect them side by side with the butterflies that represent his dreams and ideals.

The two collections, Stein seems to realize, belong together. Were it not for what the beetles represent (intolerable ugliness and a dark inevitability), there would be no need to dream of beauty—or to collect butterflies before they change, for that matter. The elusive beauty sought by the dreamer exists in as close a juxtaposition to the reality of "the Intolerable" as the rare, perfect butterfly that Stein has long been searching for exists in juxtaposition with the "heap of dirt" it is finally found resting on (210). If there were no dirt heaps—no guano islands—there would be no need to quest for the ideal or the beautiful. If there were no ugliness, there would be no thought of Paradise.

The view that although—or, more precisely, because—reality is dark we must quest for beauty and live as if our brightest ideals will last is cryptically suggested by Stein, just after Marlow has described Jim as a rare "specimen" and gone on to tell Jim's story. Stein, who seems to recognize himself in Jim, responds to Marlow's story of the young man's past history and present wanderings by saying, "I understand very well. He is romantic." As if being a romantic is having a disease that there must be some kind of medicine for, Marlow next asks Stein, "What's good for it?"

Stein goes on to say many things, nearly opaque things about "how to be," and how we "dream" of being many things we "can never be." His answer to Marlow's question, though, seems to be most comprehensibly suggested in the following famous statement:

> "Very funny this terrible thing is. A man that is born falls into a dream like a man who falls into the sea. If he tries to climb out into the air as inexperienced people endeavour to do, he drowns—*nicht wahr* [doesn't he]? . . . No! I tell you! The way is to the destructive element submit yourself, and with the exertions of your hands and feet in the water make the deep, deep sea keep you up. So, if you ask me—how to be?"
>
> His voice leaped up extraordinarily strong, as though away there in the dusk he had been inspired by some whisper of knowledge. "I will tell you! For that, too, there is only one way. . . . In the destructive element immerse." . . . He spoke in a subdued tone, without

> looking at me, one hand on each side of his face. "That was the way. To follow the dream, and again to follow the dream—and so—*ewig—usque ad finem* [eternally—and to the end]. . . .
>
> The whisper of his conviction seemed to open before me a vast and uncertain expanse. (214–15).

Marlow's apparent uncertainty as to what, exactly, he has been told in answer to his question is understandable. To be sure, it has been mirrored in the interpretive history of *Lord Jim.* Some critics have taken the phrase "the destructive element" to be a reference to a dark and painful reality—life, we might say, as represented by the beetles, not the butterflies. Others have countered with the assertion that the dream itself is the "destructive element," that which romantics must immerse themselves in if they are to respond to the question of how to be.

Odd as it may seem to define as the "destructive element" the "dream" a man "falls into"—especially given that Stein says the man "drowns" if he attempts to "climb out" of the dream—that definition seems to be the one we are most clearly led to by the text. For one thing, Stein's statement involves a deliberate confusion or reversal of terms; note that, according to Stein's analogy, we live in water and drown in air. Given that reversal, it is not entirely reasonable to assume that the destructive element would be that which drowns us. (Indeed, Stein goes on to say that the "destructive element" is *not* the air that "drowns" but, rather, the sea, in which, "with the exertions of . . . hands and feet," the dreamer makes "the deep, deep sea keep him up.")

For another thing, Stein follows up his advice to the romantic to "immerse" himself "in the destructive element" by saying that "the way" is "to follow the dream, and again to follow the dream—and so—*ewig—usque ad finem,*" eternally—and to the end. That would seem to suggest, with relative clarity, that to follow the dream—to make the quest and *not* to accept reality in all its grossness—is to immerse oneself in the destructive element. Paradoxical though it may seem, had Jim been offered and resigned himself to a future of living on a guano island and mining its dirt heap, he would *not* have immersed himself in the destructive element, in Stein's sense of those words. He would, rather, have drowned in the air that lies just beyond the sea of the romantic's dream by admitting that the world of dung—the squat and ugly world of beetles, we might say—is the only reality we have to live in.

But Jim has not "drowned" in that truth, as Old Robinson has figuratively, and as Captain Brierly has more literally. Nor is he likely to, in Stein's view, given that he is a romantic. And Stein knows Jim is a romantic, merely from hearing Marlow tell his story, because Stein, too, is a romantic and recognizes himself in Jim. That fact, alluded to earlier, is perhaps most subtly evident later in Stein's conversation with Marlow: "'He is romantic—romantic,' [Stein] repeated. 'And that is very bad—very bad. . . . Very good, too,' he added. 'But *is he?*' I queried" (216). The question clearly shows that Marlow, despite Stein's efforts to clarify that it is Jim he has been discussing, thinks Stein has been talking about himself.

Instead of straightening Marlow out about the use of pronouns, Stein goes on to tacitly admit that he *has* been talking about himself in talking about romantics. He goes on to imply, further, that Marlow, too, is a romantic—and that Marlow knows perfectly well that he is. That is why, Stein suggests, Marlow so deeply sympathizes with Jim, instead of seeing Jim as people like Chester see him—Chester who has said pointedly to Marlow, "if you could only see a thing as it is" (167). "*Gewiss*"—which means "certainly"—Stein answers, in response to Marlow's question "But *is he* [romantic]?" Continuing to "hold up the candelabrum, but without looking at me," Stein elaborates: "What is it that for you and me makes him exist?" What, in other words, if not that which you and I understand only too well, that is, his romanticism?

At "that moment," Marlow says,

> *it was difficult to believe in Jim's existence*—starting from a country parsonage, blurred by crowds of men as by clouds of dust, silenced by the clashing claims of life and death in a material world—*but his imperishable reality came to me with a convincing, with an irresistible force!* I saw vividly, as though in our progress through the

> lofty silent rooms amongst fleeting gleams of light and the sudden revelations of human figures stealing with flickering flames within unfathomable and pellucid depths, we had approached nearer to *absolute Truth,* which, *like Beauty itself, floats elusive, obscure, half submerged, in the silent still waters of mystery.* (216; emphasis added)

Marlow finally comes out of his reverie. "Perhaps he is," he admits to Stein, meaning that "perhaps Jim is a romantic." Then he continues: "but I am sure you are" (216).

And we, by reading the passage just quoted at length, can be sure *Marlow* is a romantic as well. His focus is not on the gritty, often-humble facts of temporal existence but, rather, on what he calls the "imperishable realities." His understanding of beauty not as a fleeting pleasure but, rather, as something like "absolute Truth," together with his view of beauty *and* truth as elusive, obscure, mysterious ideals or absolutes, comes straight out of Keats's "Ode on a Grecian Urn" and proves Marlow himself to be a romantic. That the indisputable realities of Jim's existence—the "country parsonage," "the crowds of men," in other words the details of his life in "a material world"—are those aspects of Jim's existence which, for Marlow, it "was *difficult* to believe in" only furthers our sense that Marlow is "romantic." That as readers we catch in the image of something half-submerged the image of something dangerous—a floating derelict, perhaps—even as Marlow uses the image to characterize the most desirable ideals only helps us to realize that being romantic can be "very bad," as well as "very good."

Marlow's dream, the goal of the particular quest he makes "with the exertions of [his] hands and feet," is faith in the nobility of human nature, in absolute moral truths, in the viability of high, fixed standards of conduct. He can find that faith if he can find Jim, someday, once again in a position of trust and respect, for Jim—to Marlow—represents the best of humanity, and Jim has made a doubt-inducing mistake. To find Jim living in some beautiful world, his greatness unquestionably established, his past behind him, would be, for Marlow, to lay to rest the ghost of that doubt that men are better than dung beetles and to reassure himself that the impossible-seeming dream he lives or "swims" in is, in fact, reality.

Jim exalted and properly adored is the elusive butterfly Marlow searches for, the specimen that proves the existence of the species, the species being a humanity capable of justifying faith in "absolute Truth" and "Beauty." Thus, the image of Jim exalted and justifiably adored is exactly what the noble identity is to Jim, who wanders the world in quest of nobility just as Marlow wanders the world in quest of Jim.

And is Jim likely to find that identity, that rare and elusive butterfly? Marlow, who follows the dream, and again and again follows the dream, as Jim follows it from the rice mill to Egstrom and Blake and then to Bangkok, seems to fear that he may not. When Stein answers his statement "I am sure you are [romantic]" with the answer "Well—I exist, too" (217), Marlow expresses that fear: "'Yes,' I said, as though carrying on a discussion, 'and amongst other things you dreamed foolishly of a certain butterfly; but when one fine morning your dream came in your way you did not let the splendid opportunity escape. Did you?'" (217). Had Jim *not jumped* from the *Patna,* Marlow suggests, he would have given permanence to his dream of heroic identity, just as Stein gave permanence to a rare butterfly's beauty by not failing to catch it up from the dirt and freeze it before it metamorphosed into something else, something ugly. But Jim did jump from the *Patna;* he completely missed his opportunity. And though Marlow doesn't know it, we know from the narrative preceding his that there have been other "fine mornings" on which the "dream" came Jim's way and, by his inaction, he failed to capture it.

But Stein, even if he knew all we as readers know, would still not be persuaded that Jim's quest is unrealizable. He is too much of a romantic. In response to Marlow's "Did you? Whereas he . . . ," Stein "lift[s] his hand. 'And do you know how many opportunities I let escape; how many dreams I had lost that had come in my way? . . . [S]ome would have been very fine.'" Marlow still has doubts: "Whether his were fine or not," he says to Stein "he knows of one which he certainly did not catch." To this, Stein responds, still unperturbed, with words that must have renewed Marlow's faith in *his* quest: "Everyone knows of one or two like that" (217).

Patusan is, for Jim, a Paradise, in that it offers a clean slate and a fresh chance. Taken there to put back into shape Stein's trading operation—which has seen better days, thanks to the inadequacies of an agent named Cornelius and to the ravages of thieves (including the royal governor, Rajah Allang, and "wild man" Sherif Ali)—Jim suddenly finds himself in a place that offers what, for him, is a perfect combination. A place of dreamy beauty, Patusan is also, with its warring factions, a place that will surely present just the kind of challenge, test, or trial Jim must have if he is to continue to be buoyed by his dream. Further, he has all the advantages he could possibly ask for in going in to face the test: to the islanders, "He appeared like a creature not only of another kind but of another essence. Had they not seen him come up in a canoe they might have thought he had descended upon them from the clouds" (229).

Jim knows what Stein has given him, too. He is almost inarticulate with gratitude on his first day there, sounding perhaps more like a humble, "below-decks" sort of hero than a hero in books. Marlow says, "this was a chance he had been dreaming of. He couldn't think how he merited that I . . . He would be shot if he could see to what he owed. . . . And it was Stein the merchant, who . . . but of course it was me he had to . . . I cut him short" (230). Later, when Marlow bids him farewell just before sailing from Patusan, during "a moment of real and profound intimacy" in which "the sort of formality that had always been present in our intercourse vanished," Jim is slightly more articulate, but not one iota less grateful. "Jove! I feel as if nothing could touch me. Why! this is luck from the word Go. I wouldn't spoil such a magnificent chance! . . . A magnificent chance!" (241).

In the allusion to Jove, in the treatment of Jim as a virtual god by the natives, and in the near-invincibility Jim feels almost from the beginning, the reader may read pride fed by circumstances that in turn will feed pride all the more. Consequently, we may finish the chapter in which Marlow leaves Patusan for the first time as fearful for Jim as

Marlow was at Stein's place, several chapters earlier. But when we return to Patusan with Marlow, one page and two years later, as we begin chapter 24, we learn that Jim, in the interim, has made only progress in his persistent attempts to follow and find the dream, the elusive butterfly of a noble, heroic identity.

He has made that progress, moreover, by doing deeds of real bravery and even gallantry. The man who, according to Chester, might not have felt cowardice on a guano island with twin six-shooters at his disposal had, early on, surrendered the revolver Marlow had given him, on being taken prisoner by Tunku Allang. Rather than cowering with fear, Jim had "Resolutely, coolly, and for some time enlarged" for the rajah "on the text that no man should be prevented from getting his food and his children's shelter honestly" (250). Shortly after taking that "risk," and after facing a new, non-European inquiry ("Were the Dutch coming to take the country? Would the white man like to go back down the river? What was the object of coming?"), Jim had escaped the rajah and his men and found Doramin, the elected "chief of the second power in Patusan," the Bugis, "immigrants from the Celebes" who "formed the party opposed to the Rajah" (251, 256). Jim had immediately befriended Doramin, his old wife, and, especially, their son—much as Stein had earlier gone to the Celebes themselves and befriended Mohammed Bonso, son of the queen of the Wajo States.

The Bugis, or Celebes immigrants, had for years been involved in "quarrels" with the rajah over "trade," in "faction fights" whose "sudden outbreaks . . . would fill this or that part of the settlement with smoke, flame, the noise of shots and shrieks." And for years they had been getting the worst of the quarrels. "Villages" had been "burnt," and men had been "dragged into the Rajah's stockade to be killed or tortured" (256–57). The only chance the Bugis had had of standing up to the thieving, torturing rajah had involved forming an unacceptable alliance with Sherif Ali and his men. Nonetheless, "The younger spirits" among the Celebes immigrants, "chaffing, advised to 'get Sherif Ali with his wild men and drive the Rajah Allang out of the country'" (257–58).

That had been "the state of affairs when Jim, bolting from the rajah's stockade," had "appeared before the chief of the Bugis," produced the ring [sent by Stein]," and been "received . . . into the heart of the community" (258). Soon after, things had changed dramatically. Working with Dain Waris, the chief's son, Jim had helped the Bugis launch an entirely successful attack on Sherif Ali's heretofore-"impregnable" hilltop camp (263). Having "induced the war party to work all night," Jim had "improvised a rude capstan out of a hollowed log" and figured out a way to use it, plus cables, to drag "Doramin's old ordnance" to "the top of that hill; two rusty iron 7-pounders, a lot of small brass cannon" (263). Not long after, "the defeated Sherif Ali" had "fled the country," and, "as to old Tunku Allang, his fears at first had known no bounds." As Jim tells Marlow: "It is said that at the intelligence of the successful storming of the hill [Allang] flung himself, face down, on the bamboo floor of his audience-hall, and lay motionless for a whole night and a whole day, uttering stifled sounds of such an appalling nature that no man dared approach his prostrate form nearer than a spear's length. . . . After Sherif Ali his turn would come, and who could resist an attack led by such a devil?" (273)

If to Rajah Allang Jim had shown himself to be a devil, to the Bugis he had shown himself to be nothing less than Tuan, or "Lord," Jim. By the time of Marlow's return, after two years' absence, Jim "was like a figure set up on a pedestal, to represent in his persistent youth the power, and perhaps the virtues, of races that never grow old, that have emerged from the gloom" (265). He *is*, in a sense, the standard of conduct by which others are judged: "they had got into the habit of taking his word for anything and everything," Marlow later tells his audience, not long after leaving the island again; "Only the other day an old fool he had never seen in his life came from some village miles away to find out if he should divorce his wife" (268). On trial at inquiries earlier, Jim is now far enough along in his quest to himself be the magistrate. As Marlow tells it, affecting Jim's conversation, "Could settle the deadliest quarrel in the country by crooking his little finger. The trouble was to get at the truth of anything. Was not sure to this day whether he had been fair to all parties. It worried him" (269).

As a result (and as seeming proof) of Jim's magisterial if not lordly status, he has won the love of a "girl" with "delicate features and a profound, attentive glance" (278). She is the daughter of a woman who, before her death, had been married to Cornelius, the "awful Malacca Portuguese" who had served as Stein's first trader in Patusan. Jim, who "had a . . . romantic conscience," has named the girl Jewel to signify her spiritual value to him (276). "You know—this," he tells the visiting Marlow, "no confounded nonsense about it—can't tell you how much I owe to her" (278).

In gaining Jewel, Jim has gained something priceless, for she is "as much of a woman" as her mother was, and her mother, Stein has told Marlow, "was no ordinary woman" (277, 276). Jewel's "tenderness," which "hovered over [Jim] like a flutter of wings," as well as her "vigilant affection" with an "intensity . . . almost perceptible," solidifies the self-image Jim is ever in search of. Only a noble man, after all, would be worthy of them (283).

"Romance," Marlow says, "had singled Jim for its own—and that was the true part of the story. . . . He did not hide his jewel. In fact, he was extremely proud of it" (282). But the truth is, romance has not singled Jim out. Rather, the "romantic" has sought out romance. In following his dream, Jim has stood up to rajahs and ascended to impenetrable fortresses and now reached the point on his quest where he has won a human jewel in that crown which may finally signify the attainment of the end of his quest.

7

After the Quest: The Truth?

If Jewel, by her very name, seems to signify attainment and thus perhaps the goal or near-end of Jim's quest, she is, at the same time, the innocent beginning of new troubles for Jim—troubles that will eventually jeopardize her lover's quest for a new and noble identity and self-image in Patusan.

Marlow first hears of dangers connected with Jewel's name as he puts into a port "about 230 miles south" of where Jim lives. There Marlow meets some kind of "third-class deputy assistant agent," a "big, fat, greasy, blinking fellow of mixed descent," who asks him, "Going to Patusan?" Hearing that Marlow is, the man goes on to comment that "There's some sort of white vagabond has got in there, I hear." When Marlow realizes the man is talking about Jim and consequently warns the agent that the so-called vagabond is his friend, the fat man says something that only later comes to make sense to Marlow: "Well, then, . . . if he has really got hold of something good—none of your bits of green glass—understand?—I am a government official—you tell the rascal . . . I am pleased to give you the hint. I suppose you, too, would like to get something out of it? Don't interrupt. You just tell him I've heard the tale, but to my government I have made no report. . . . Understand? I know some good people that will buy anything worth having, and can give him more money than the scoundrel ever saw in his life. I know his sort" (279). The news that a white man has "Found his way in" to Patusan and, beyond that, "got hold of" a "Jewel" has become the rumor that a "white vagabond" has gone into a land where "they cut throats" and found himself a jewel of great price (279). A woman's figurative name has not traveled very far "south of the Patusan river," in other words, before becoming what ordinary people would prefer it to be: a word literally signifying the nearby presence of a bit of earth worth cutting throats for (278).

And the news doesn't stop there. "Next day," Marlow says, ". . . I discovered that a story was traveling slowly down the coast about a mysterious white man in Patusan who had got hold of an extraordinary gem—namely, an emerald of an enormous size, and altogether priceless. . . . The white man had obtained it, I was told, partly by the exercise of his wonderful strength and partly by cunning, from the ruler of a distant country, whence he had fled instantly, arriving in Patusan in utmost distress, but frightening the people by his extreme ferocity, which nothing seemed able to subdue" (280). From "a sort of scribe to the wretched little Rajah of the place" in which he has met the fat government agent, Marlow hears "this amazing Jim-myth" in its fully blossomed version. "'[S]uch a jewel,'" the scribe explains to him, "'is best preserved by being concealed about the person of a woman. Yet it is not every woman that would do. She must be young'—he sighed deeply—'and insensible to the seductions of love.'" The man says he has been told of "a tall girl, whom the white man treated with great respect and care, and who never went forth from the house unattended. . . . [T]here could be no doubt she wore the white man's jewel concealed upon her bosom" (280–81). The young woman named Jewel who has nothing but Jim, whom she loves above all else, has been turned, as language has passed from one mind to another, into a girl who is immune to love and who has a jewel on her person.

Perhaps for this reason, during the period Jim lives across the river from Doramin's place with Jewel and her father, Cornelius, Jim comes to feel "all sorts of dangers gathering obscurely about him." Almost nightly, people he is unfamiliar with call on him at home, "often in the dead of night, in order to disclose to him plots for his assassination." Some say he is to be poisoned; others warn him plans are afoot to have him stabbed "in the bath-house"; still others say he is going to be shot at by someone on a boat plying the river. "Each of these informants," Jim tells Marlow, "professed himself to be his very good friend. It was enough . . . to spoil a fellow's rest for ever" (290).

Among the self-professed friends who would warn Jim of accumulating dangers is Jewel's father, Cornelius himself. Cornelius almost certainly does not believe Jim to be in possession of any jewel other than his daughter, but he, too, seems to want to spoil Jim's rest, frighten him into believing he is in danger, and, in the process, get him to leave Patusan. In "solemn, wheedling tones" Cornelius tells his impressive replacement of a plan whereby Jim may, figuratively speaking, jump ship: run away from Patusan as the *Patna*'s skipper ran away from the inquiry; drop out of dangerous conditions as quickly and suddenly as Brierly dropped out of life itself. For "one hundred dollars—or even for eighty; let's say eighty—he, Cornelius, would procure a trustworthy man to smuggle Jim out of the river, all safe" (290). Whereas Brierly once offered 100 rupees to help Jim escape, Cornelius will make it *possible* for him to run away in *exchange* for 100—make that 80—dollars.

Cornelius, described in one place as a man whose "walk resembled the creeping of a repulsive beetle" and in another as a "skulking" man whose "loathsomeness" was such that "a merely disgusting person would have appeared noble by his side," sees Jim as a rival (285–86). Not only is he jealous of the fact that Jim is poised to be a more successful agent for Stein than he ever was; not only is he jealous of the fact that Jim has been, from the beginning, worshiped as little less than a god; but he is also jealous because of Jim's love for his daughter and, especially, because of her love for Jim.

Cornelius, we are told, has long "insisted upon her calling him father—'and with respect, too—with respect,' he would scream. . . .

'Your mother was a devil, a deceitful devil—and you, too, are a devil,' he would shriek" (288). The passage, found near the beginning of chapter 30, is not the first to indicate that Cornelius is not Jewel's biological father. At the beginning of the previous chapter, we had been told that "Cornelius . . . nursed the aggrieved sense of his legal paternity," meaning that he knew himself not to be his daughter's biological parent (282).

That Cornelius is *not* Jewel's biological parent—that Jewel is the daughter of the wife who gave herself to someone else—opens up interesting interpretive possibilities. We may be able to explain Cornelius's overinsistence on the love and respect of Jewel by suggesting that the girl represents a double of the mother and, thus, a second chance to hold onto something Cornelius lost when his wife gave herself to another man. That Jewel is a beautiful woman biologically unrelated to Cornelius only widens the possibility that the desire not to lose her to another man is, at root, sexual desire and jealousy, masked as an extreme form of a more typical, paternal love and desire not to lose a daughter.

There may be, moreover, an even more significant element in the makeup of the jealousy Cornelius feels as he sees Jim express love for Jewel and receive it in return: namely, the true biological paternity of the girl Jim calls Jewel. When Marlow first went to Stein to see about getting help for Jim, Stein had pointed to a map of Patusan. "There's Patusan," he had said. "And the woman is dead now," he had "added incomprehensibly" (219). Marlow goes on to say that "The only woman that had ever existed for him was the Malay girl he called 'My wife the princess,' or, more rarely in moments of expansion, 'the mother of my Emma.'" Marlow continues:

> Who was the woman he had mentioned in connection with Patusan I can't say; but from his allusions I understand she had been an educated and very good-looking Dutch-Malay girl, with a tragic or perhaps only a pitiful history, whose most painful part no doubt was her marriage with a Malacca Portuguese. . . . It was solely for his wife's sake that Stein had appointed him manager of Stein & Co.'s trading post in Patusan; but commercially the arrangement

> was not a success, at any rate for the firm, and now the woman had died, Stein was disposed to try another agent there. (219–20)

The Malacca Portuguese, the man Jim was sent to "relieve," was, of course, the man "whose name was Cornelius." Marlow says "it is impossible to suspect Stein" of anything untoward with Cornelius's wife, because "The only woman that had ever existed for him was the Malay . . . mother of [his] Emma," and Stein's wife was a "Dutch-Malay" girl. But Marlow also admits that "Patusan had been used as a grave for some sin, transgression, or misfortune," and Marlow's refusal to believe that Stein had been Cornelius's wife's lover and therefore the transgressor may be more of a symptom of his own idealistic nature than of anything else.

Of course, even if we believe that Stein *is* a man with whom Cornelius's wife was once unfaithful, that doesn't mean he is Jewel's biological father. "I don't think [Cornelius] will go away from the place," Stein tells Marlow, on deciding to replace Cornelius with Jim. "[A]s I think there is a daughter left, I shall let him, if he likes to stay, keep the old house" (220). If Jewel is Stein's daughter, would he refer to her as "a" daughter? Is that perhaps *why* he calls her "a"—not "my"—daughter? And if she isn't his daughter, would he have let Cornelius keep the house?

These questions are all the more powerful and suggestive because the novel provides us with no easy answers to them. They urge, almost force, us to indulge in complex speculations, each of which leads us to conclude that dangers are gathering around Jim—without quite being sure that they are or, if they are, why. If Cornelius once lost his wife to his dashing, heroic boss and is now losing the child he fathered with her—a child he loves with a jealous, perhaps sexual love—to the dashing, heroic, reputedly divine young man whom his old boss has sent to take over his old employment, then he has multiple reasons to see Jim as a dangerous rival. Add to Cornelius's complexly motivated jealousy the fact that he is a skulking, unusually disgusting, loathsome person, and it is easy to feel he is as potentially dangerous to Jim as is the rumor that Jim possesses a priceless stone.

Those dangers become increasingly apparent from chapter 30 on. When Jim politely refuses, once and for all, Cornelius's offer to smuggle him secretly out of Patusan, the response of Stein's deposed agent is telling: "'Your blood be on your own head,' he squeaked" (291). Not long after, lying on his mat and hearing "stealthy footsteps" outside on the veranda, Jim hears "A voice whisper[ing] tremulously through the wall, 'Are you asleep?'" He rushes outside to find Cornelius, who asks, "Have you given your consideration to what I spoke to you about?" When Jim responds by saying, "I am going to live here, in Patusan," Cornelius responds with, "You shall d-d-die h-h-here" (292–93).

The very next night, Jim almost does die in Patusan. His "slumbers" are "disturbed" by what he at first thinks is a dream—one in which a voice is calling him to "Awake!" by the light of the "glare of a red fluttering conflagration"—that turns out to be Jewel with a torch. "Get up!" she urges him, handing him a revolver and leading him out of the room onto the veranda, where the hammock Cornelius normally sleeps in swings empty. From the house—one of four buildings in a compound—Jewel leads him out into the courtyard, telling him as they go that he was to have been killed while he slept. "They are in the storeroom waiting, . . . waiting for the signal," she tells him, referring to Sherif Ali's emissaries. Jim asks her, "Who's to give it?" and, shortly thereafter, gets his answer in the form of a rustle in the grass. "Something dark, imperfectly seen, flitted rapidly out of sight. He called out in a strong voice, 'Cornelius! O Cornelius!'" The narration continues: "'Fly!' she said. . . . 'Fly!' repeated the girl, excitedly. 'They are frightened now—this light—the voices. They know you are awake now—they know you are big, strong, fearless. . . .' 'If I am all that,' he began, but she interrupted him. 'Yes—tonight! But what of to-morrow night? Of the next night? Of the night after—of all the many, many nights? Can I always be watching?' A sobbing catch of her breath affected him beyond the power of words." Marlow, in telling the story, says that Jim later told him "he had never felt so small, so powerless—and as to courage, what was the good of it?" (298–99).

Jim's quest for courage and for the heroic identity that requires and is defined by it seems to be momentarily derailed by the knowledge that he would not even be alive had a young woman not been staying up night after night, watching while he slept. Nonetheless, disconcerted though he is by this realization and despite Jewel's advice that he fly to Doramin's, Jim strides to the storeroom, violently pushes open the door, raises his weapon, and finds himself "exchanging glances with a pair of eyes" in "a heap of mats." Suddenly, "the whole mound stirred, and with a low grunt a man emerged swiftly, and bounded towards Jim" (301). Holding his shot, Jim lets the man come at him, firing and killing only when he has to. Another man then threatens Jim, but suddenly thinks better of it, casting aside the spear he has pointed at Jim. "You want your life?" Jim asks (302). Three men crawl out of the darkness and are led, past their dead accomplice, out of the storeroom. "Take my greetings to Sherif Ali," Jim says, freeing the men to return to him who has sent them. It is on this very night that Jim develops his plan to assault Ali and drive him out of the country.

Marlow hears these stories, both of Jim's bravery and of the growing dangers to his friend, on his second visit to Patusan—the same visit on which he meets Jewel. Having already come to wonder if Jim isn't endangered by the rumor that the young woman named Jewel is, literally speaking, a jewel of great price, he comes quickly to sense that danger lies in Jewel's father, Cornelius, as well. Finally, in a scene thoroughly demonstrative of Cornelius's repulsiveness, Marlow comes to realize that Jewel and jewel, literal and figurative, come together in Cornelius's sick mind: to Cornelius, Jewel is a thing, a possession, something for which he ought to be compensated monetarily if he is to lose her to another owner. When he realizes that Marlow is not going to intercede and talk Jim into paying for safe passage out of Patusan, he stutters out, "Moderate provision—suitable present." The old man seemed, Marlow suddenly realizes, "to be claiming value for something, and he even went the length of saying with some warmth that life was not worth having if a man were to be robbed of everything. I did not breathe a word, of course, but neither did I stop my ears. The gist of the affair, which became clear to me gradually, was in this, that *he regarded himself as entitled to some money in exchange for the girl.* He had brought her up. Somebody else's child. Great trouble and pains—old man now—suitable present" (327–28; emphasis added). According to the terms of Cornelius's twisted logic, if he gets no monetary payoff for his investment, Jim will be a thief who has made off with a treasure—and deserving of no more and no less than what such thieves get.

As Marlow comes to realize the dangers impinging on Jim, he also comes to realize that, in Jewel's view, Marlow himself is the greatest threat or danger of all, for although Jewel has selflessly urged Jim to leave, seeing how bent his enemies are on killing him, Jim's departure is the thing that, deep down, she most fears, and Marlow's presence obviously intensifies that fear. "I belonged," as Marlow puts it, "to this Unknown that might claim Jim for its own at any moment. . . . I believe she supposed I could with a word whisk Jim away out of her very arms" (308). When she privately puts that fear into words, Marlow protests that he has come with "no intention to take Jim away," but Jewel asks the question once again. Marlow says he persisted in trying "to explain briefly: friendship, business. . . ." But "'They always leave us,' she murmured" (309).

Taking pity on the young woman, Marlow explains that Jim will never break his word to her by leaving Patusan. "Fear shall never drive him away," he assures her, to which she responds by saying that Jim has been trying to tell her something—something of a past she does not understand. Jewel is tortured, both by the desire to know and by the competing desire not to know the details of Jim's life before this life, and it is easy to guess at the nature of her terrible ambivalence. On one hand, the life he has led before coming to her is part of that great unknown, part of that mystery, that might cause him to leave her, despite his declared intentions. If he has been a great man who has been missed and is wanted back, he may have obligations higher than his love for her. On the other hand, what if his shrouded past has not been one of bravery, of greatness? If he has, in his past life, shown a fear or weakness that she has never seen since his arrival in Patusan, and if he should show that same fear or weakness again, the result might be his running away with Marlow. Either way, his past raises the omen of his departure: the thing she most fears for her own sake.

Jewel remembers that a man like Jim left her mother behind: a man that, we may speculate, might have been Stein. "You all remember something!" she says to Marlow. "You all go back to it. What is it? You tell me! What is this thing? Is it alive?—is it dead? I hate it. It is cruel. . . . Will he see it—will he hear it? In his sleep perhaps when he cannot see me—and then arise and go. Ah! I shall never forgive him. My mother had forgiven—but I, never! Will it be a sign—a call?" (315). If Marlow suspects that Stein was the man who heard the call and left, he also knows that this romantic's great love was someone other than Jewel's mother. By contrast, Marlow can see clearly that Jewel is part of Jim's dream, part of what sustains him in his quest for a noble identity. "She owned, as I . . . put it to her, his heart. She had that and everything else—if she could only believe it. What I had to tell her was that in the whole world there was no one who ever would need his heart, his mind, his hand" (317). From beyond the horizon, "From all the multitudes that peopled the vastness of that unknown . . . neither a call nor a sign for him" will come, Marlow assures Jewel.

That revelation leads to one of the most important moments in the book, for Jewel can hardly believe that, whatever else has happened, Jim has been what we might call a beetle and not a butterfly. He, after all, cannot possibly be the kind of man her legal father, Cornelius, is, the kind who would be unwanted out in that vast "Unknown" from which white-skinned sailors arrive by ship. When in Jewel's look Marlow beholds "the protest of an invincible unbelief," he responds to it with more questions. "Why should she fear? She knew him to be strong, true, wise, brave. He was all that. Certainly. He was more. He was great, invincible—and the world did not want him. . . . 'Why?' she murmured. I felt that sort of rage one feels during a hard tussle. The spectre was trying to slip out of my grasp. 'Why?' she repeated louder; 'tell me!' And as I remained confounded she stamped her foot like a spoilt child. 'Why? Speak.' 'You want to know?' I asked in a fury. 'Yes!' she cried. 'Because he is not good enough,' I said brutally" (318). Jewel, though she first admits that "This is the very thing [Jim] said," nonetheless goes on to cry out at Marlow, in her native dialect, words meaning "You lie!" Marlow tries to explain as she catches her breath and flings his arm away: "Nobody, nobody is good enough." (318–19).

Marlow's statement—that "nobody is good enough"—can be read in a number of (almost-conflicting) ways, as can the whole last portion of Conrad's novel. Most positively, it could mean that Jim is as good as any human being who has ever lived—that he has been judged, in other words, unfairly and even absurdly. He is the great and innocent victim of a society that has made a terrible mistake. He is not good enough, and he is not wanted back because he is not good enough; then again, if *he* is not good enough, *no one* is, for he is at least as great as Jewel believes him to be, and that is magnificent indeed.

Most negatively, it could mean that Marlow has now seen that Jim is—in the words of Chester, the owner of the guano island—no good at all. Since Marlow has formerly and long seen Jim as the best of humanity, he has concluded, therefore, that humanity itself is no good. Jim is merely human and, consequently, will continue to be frail and vulnerable, prone to yet another abysmal failure. Read this way, Marlow's comment would have to mean that his own quest for belief in heroism has come to an end. Marlow has ceased to believe, according to this reading, in the possibility of what in an earlier chapter we termed difference, or *differents*. If "nobody is good enough," then everyone is more or less the same, and Jim's romantic dream to the contrary is but a dream—whether or not circumstances prove it to be one.

There is another way of reading Marlow's comment: a way at once more pessimistic than the first reading and more optimistic than the second. Marlow could mean that Jim probably *is* exceptionally good. Marlow tells Jewel, after all, that Jim is strong, true, wise, and brave—as Jewel believes him to be. In saying that Jim is not good enough, because no one is *ever* good enough, Marlow could be saying that time inevitably presents some great heroes with a test they cannot pass. That doesn't mean, though, that humankind shouldn't have demanding, even impossibly high ideals of behavior.

It is a characteristic of the race, in other words, to dream dreams, define ideals, and fix standards of conduct so impossibly demanding that, finally, all human beings—no matter how noble—fall short of them. According to this third reading, some of the noblest of people, like Jim, are inevitably the victims of what we might call collective romanticism. Once proved by circumstance to be short of the ideal that has been set by the collective imagination, they are left to lead out the rest of their noble lives in a place that, because it is beyond the margins or boundaries of the society whose ideals they have fallen short of, serves to reassert the belief that the ideal is attainable. Otherwise, why would those who have failed to attain it be banished there?

That process of banishing (in its most extreme instances, scapegoating) a few in order to maintain the ideals of the many may be unpleasant, in that it produces individual human victims. It may be immoral, and even the very source of tragedy, which otherwise would be unknown as a condition, let alone as a literary genre. But it may also be necessary if *humanity,* as a collective romantic being, is to continue to follow the dream, continue to immerse itself in the destructive element, continue to believe in the reality of that sea which keeps us from drowning in the air of reality.

This third reading of Marlow's comment—and of the ending of *Lord Jim*—steers a careful course between most of the readings to be found in the extant criticism: readings that, on one hand, would insist on Jim's (and through Jim's, Marlow's) ultimate greatness and triumph, and that, on the other, would see him as a dismal failure and Marlow either as a fool for continuing to believe in his goodness, even greatness, or as a disillusioned man whose romantic bubbles have all, by the end of the story, been appropriately burst. And yet, judicious as this third reading is, we must recognize that there is much in the novel following the description of Marlow's departure to justify the darkest possible reading of Jim and of the romanticism he stands for.

Before examining such reasons, it might be helpful to review the events of the story's end—and the way they are learned and made known. Shortly after hearing Cornelius suggest that he deserves a "suitable present" in exchange for Jewel, Marlow leaves Patusan for the last time, to return to his life of sailing—and storytelling. Two years after Marlow has told his audience about his recent departure from Jim, one former listener—called "the privileged man" by the omniscient narrator who narrates the beginning of chapter 36—receives a package addressed to him in Marlow's hand (337). The package contains a letter from Marlow, an unfinished piece of writing by Jim, a letter to Jim from his father, and, most important, a handwritten narrative by Marlow telling what he has learned of Jim's end in his travels since leaving Patusan.

The writings by Jim and his father tell little; the letter from Marlow basically states that in Bangkok he met a dying man, known as Gentleman Brown, eight months after having learned of Jim's death at Stein's place, where he had met a distraught Jewel and a disillusioned Tamb' Itam. But Marlow's narrative to the "privileged man" has much to say, if only implicitly and indirectly, both to the reader and to "the privileged man" who himself is also a reader (and who, perhaps like us, has always suspected that Jim would have been better off staying and "fighting in the ranks," however humbly, of his own critical and judgmental society [339]).

Marlow's narrative tells its privileged readers, first of all, that the "Gentleman" named Brown whose arrival in Patusan spelled the beginning of Jim's end, the push preceding what was perhaps yet another fall, was humanity's ultimate "beetle": a pirate, thief, kidnapper, and all-around terrorist. Brown had gone to Patusan not only because he had heard it was ripe for the picking but also because, in his stolen ship, he hadn't wanted to dock at any more "civilized" port. There he had been attacked downriver from the Bugis, not far from the rajah's stockade, where he and his "fourteen desperate invaders" had built fortifications out of "felled trees" (360). There, too, he had been helped by the traitor Cornelius—who had brought him and his men supplies and advice—and been hemmed in by Dain Waris. (With Jim away in the interior, the son of Doramin had decided to lead a band of men downriver and set up camp on an island below the terrorists, thereby effectively blocking the bandits' retreat.)

Jim, on returning to the Bugis, had heard of the situation and gone immediately to Gentleman Brown, who "hated Jim at first sight" (380). Seeing Jim as a hypocrite who had probably come to Patusan because of some crime as bad as those he himself committed, Brown appealed to Jim's fear that the two of them were brothers in imperfection. "You talk as if you were one of those people that should have wings so as to go about without touching the dirty earth," Brown says mockingly to Jim, recalling pointedly for us, in the process, the butterfly/beetle symbolism of chapter 20. "Well—it is dirty," Brown continues. "I haven't got any wings. I am here because of? A prison. That scares me, and you may know it—if it's any good to you. I won't ask you what scared you into this infernal hole, where you seem to have found pretty pickings" (383). "He then asked Jim," Marlow writes, "whether he had nothing fishy in his life to remember that he was so damnedly hard upon a man trying to get out of a deadly hole. . . . And there ran through the rough talk a vein of subtle reference to their common blood, an assumption of common experience; a sickening suggestion of common guilt, of secret knowledge that was like a bond of their minds and of their hearts" (387). Jim, consequently, and no doubt as a result of Brown's talk, asks his dark opposite, or, some would say, alter ego, if he will promise to give up his arms and leave for the coast. Hearing Brown say he is not "crazy" enough to leave himself and his men unprotected, Jim says, "suddenly after a long silence, 'Very well. . . . You shall have a clear road or else a clear fight'" (388).

Instead, told by Cornelius "another way out of the river" that leads to the back side of the island that Dain Waris and his men are on, Brown "retreats" and, on his way, starts anything but a "clear" fight. "Stealthily he landed his men on the other side of the island opposite to the Bugis camp, and led them across. . . . When he judged the moment come, Brown yelled, 'Let them have it,' and fourteen shots rang out like one. . . . Dain Waris . . . ran out upon the open shore, just in time to receive a bullet in his forehead" (403–4). When the body of Dain Waris reaches Doramin's house, Jim goes immediately to his friend's father, who has "let out one great fierce cry, deep from the chest, a roar of pain and fury" (411). "I am come in sorrow," he says to Doramin; ". . . I am come ready and unarmed." Then, "while Jim stood stiffened and with bared head . . . , [Doramin] clung heavily with his left arm round the neck of a bowed youth, and lifting deliberately his right, shot his son's friend through the chest" (415–16).

Marlow ends his narrative describing Jim as "inscrutable at heart, forgotten, unforgiven, and excessively romantic." Do we end up feeling that romanticism is good? Can it be good, if it is excessive? And what about what Marlow goes on to say on the novel's last page—"Not in the wildest days of his boyish visions could he have seen the alluring shape of such an extraordinary success"? Has Jim succeeded in his quest in the moment he bravely submits himself to be shot by Doramin? Does *he* believe he has, or does he die in hopelessness and despair, his death a suicide in all but name only? What was his quest for, if it was successfully concluded in the moment the bullet tore through his chest? And is Marlow being straight with us when he calls Jim's end a success? Or is he being bitterly ironic? Note how he continues: "[Jim] goes away from a living woman to celebrate his pitiless wedding with a shadowy ideal of conduct" (416).

And there are questions antecedent even to these questions. Why did Jim give Brown free passage with weapons? Did he do so because, in his romantic idealism, he wanted to believe the best of Brown and give the man another chance, even as he has long wanted to believe the best of himself and have the benefit of a new start? Or was it because Brown's accusatory speeches made him feel no better than the worst of men and, therefore, a fraud in treating punitively a man no worse than himself? Marlow concludes his narrative with an answer to one of these many questions that is really no answer at all. And yet it could stand as the answer to all of them: "We ought to know. He is one of us" (416).

The notion that Conrad's novel ultimately believes, if not in the character of Jim, then in humanity, its ideals, and its potential for nobility depends largely on the fact that it ends with questions it allows us to answer. In other words, the idea, advanced a few pages earlier, that *Lord Jim* does not end on a despairing note (whether or not Lord Jim does) is implied by the fact that it ends with questions we are challenged, even trusted, to answer.

Had Conrad been confirmed in nihilism, convinced that there is no success distinguishable from failure, no possibility of difference and, therefore, of human *differents,* his text would surely have left less, if any, room for debate or creative speculation. He would have foreclosed the debate that has, in fact, characterized commentary on the novel ever since its publication. Rather than leaving us to quest for truth on our own, challenging us (much as "the privileged man" is challenged by Marlow) to test, prove, or possibly change our beliefs in light of the experience of the text, Conrad would simply have told us—drily, cynically, and via an incontestably omniscient narrator—about a monotonous world of inherently flawed inhabitants.

Instead, Conrad abandons omniscience and his seemingly omniscient narrator just five chapters into the novel. He attempts, at least implicitly, to explain the change in point of view in his "Author's Note" to the 1917 edition, saying that he had at first intended the novel to be "a short story, concerned only with the pilgrim ship episode, nothing more," but had later perceived that episode to be "a good starting point for a free and wandering tale" (viii). But we can speculate that Conrad may have abandoned writing a straightforward, omniscient narrative about the abandonment of the *Patna* because it suggested too limited a view of human nature and possibility; similarly, we can speculate that he let the story continue in the uncertain, searching words of Marlow precisely to allow for the possibility of wider definitions, at least in the "free and wandering" minds of some readers.

To allow for that possibility and to allow us that imaginative freedom, Conrad delivers Jim's tale via a man who is himself like us, if not one of us. Not a reader, Marlow *is* nonetheless in a position analogous to that of a reader; he is first described as a "listener" at the inquiry, and his struggle to gain truth from Jim's story mirrors and validates our struggle to make sense of his narrative. Of course, we no more have the luxury of getting *all* of Jim's story from Marlow—whose idiosyncrasies we may come to feel we know—than Marlow has the luxury of getting it all from Jim. Part of what reaches us *through* Marlow has its sources in narrators as various as Tamb' Itam and Gentleman Brown. And this same information not only originates with persons other than Marlow but is also passed on by Marlow to us via "the privileged man." (Presumably, according to the internal logic of the fiction, "the privileged man" could have kept private the contents of the package Marlow sent him after Jim's death. That was, presumably, part of his privilege—even as it was his privilege to relay Marlow's narrative to others like us.)

The presence of "the privileged man" as an intermediary between (a) the reader and (b) Marlow and his sources only raises more open-ended questions about the text we hold in our hands, the vehicle we must take in our individual quests, as readers, for meaning or our own version of truth. Who is it who, throughout the novel, says things like "the privileged man opened the packet, looked in, then, laying it down, went to the window"? Who says, at the beginning of chapter 36, "It came to him at home, more than two years later, and it came contained in a thick packet addressed in Marlow's upright and angular handwriting" (337)? Can we be sure that it is not "the privileged man" himself? Can we be sure that, according to the internal logic of the fiction, he is not the "outside" narrator narrating from page one on? What we assumed was an omnisciently narrated opening suddenly comes to seem almost its own opposite. We can hardly reconcile the idea of omniscience with the idea that the outside narrator of *Lord Jim* is, in fact, the one narrator who witnessed none of the action and who indeed was the last person before us to receive the tale.

This is but one example of the myriad ways in which the text surprises and even confuses us, violates—or, to use the language of the novel, *checks*—our conventionally conditioned expectations as readers in ways that test us, make us think, and challenge us to act interpretively in an imaginative manner. Another of the ways in which the text makes us quest for meaning rather than simply receive it passively is by presenting events achronologically. We are at the trial *be-*

fore hearing about Jim's jump; we read about the experience of the French lieutenant *before* we read about the conclusion of the inquiry, a fact that does not seem to violate chronological law until we consider that Marlow didn't learn about the French lieutenant's experience until "more than three years" had passed (149). One result of Conrad's achronological presentation is that sometimes we are given information before we can figure out how to apply it—or even to make sense of it. At other times we are made to wait to learn fully about an event we know, or at least suspect, has happened, the result being that our understanding of the world of the text is always qualified by a certain uncertainty.

At its extreme, the result of the text's achronology is uncertainty, on our part as readers, as to who is talking, who is being talked about, or to whom a given pronoun refers. Chapter 8, for instance, ends this way: "He could no more stop telling now than he could have stopped living by the mere exertion of his will" (100). Chapter 9, then, begins as follows: "'I was saying to myself, "Sink—curse you!"'" But whereas the "he" at the end of chapter 8 refers to Jim, Jim is the "'I'" referred to at the beginning of chapter 9. If we are to make our interpretive way smoothly and safely across the passage between the two chapters, we will have to be alert and ready to notice, without guidance from an omniscient narrator, the subtlest of details, such as the sequence of quotation marks surrounding a pronoun.

The achronology of the text and the complex narrative structure, both of which contribute to our need to continually think about such things as pronoun reference, put us simultaneously on our own yet also among a group of searchers for meaning—not unlike those individuals within a group who sit listening to Marlow, simultaneously together yet also each separated by a "dusk" as "deep" as the sea. Indeed, the complexity of the text's narrative structure and chronology is *like* the darkness in which the members of Marlow's audience sit, unable to see clearly their narrator as he speaks or, for that matter, the scene about them, including as it does the other listeners.

> Marlow showed himself willing to remember Jim, to remember him at length, in detail and audibly.

> Perhaps it would be after dinner, on a verandah, draped in motionless foliage and crowned with flowers, in the deep dusk speckled by fiery cigar-ends. The elongated bulk of each cane chair harboured a silent listener. Now and then a small red glow would move abruptly, and expanding light up the fingers of a languid hand, part of a face in profound repose, or flash a crimson gleam into a pair of pensive eyes overshadowed by a fragment of an unruffled forehead; and with the very first word uttered Marlow's body, extended at rest in the seat, would become very still, as though his spirit had winged its way back into the lapse of time and were speaking through his lips from the past. (33)

The "part of a face" here, "flash" of "crimson there," and "fragment of an unruffled forehead" further on that Marlow's listeners experience as they sit, alone together in the "elongated bulk" of their chairs, is by extension like the jumbled, fragmentary nature of the reading experience that all readers must piece together on their own. The complexity of the text is, after all, figuratively an *obscurity,* analogous to the literal obscurity of the kind isolating Marlow's listeners. It forces us to shed our own light in and on the almost-all-engulfing darkness.

Paradoxically, the isolating obscurity can be read positively. Through its pictures of audiences isolated in a single deep duskiness, the text causes us to feel a kinship with others struggling but also trusted to deliberate about and decide on what is true, based on fragments unrelated to one another by direct authorial narration. That feeling of kinship, connected as it is with a trust in the power of the individual to quest for truth, is, of course, arguably unrealistic: it seems to be idealistic, even—as Stein might say—romantic.

That same paradoxical idealism can, further, be read in any number of the novel's characteristics that, on the surface, would seem darkly suggestive. Take the interfacing of places and times and narratives—the fact that Jim's narrative as repeated by Marlow is interrupted by other narrators and by references to Marlow's narration to an audience. That apparent confusion or even chaos could be seen as implying a potential for human beings to interpenetrate and know one another—an implication that directly contradicts the novel's readily quotable statement that each of us swims in our own separate sea without hope of successful emergence and, therefore, of communication.

These paradoxical counterstatements, to be sure, remain unresolved; the novel is, admittedly, quiet in stating its faith in the possibility of understanding and representing the truth—and of having it comprehended. Indeed, sometimes it seems to go in the other direction, dramatizing inarticulateness (as in the following passage, in which Jim speaks to Marlow):

> He stood stock-still, as if struck motionless by a discovery. "You have given me confidence," he declared, soberly. "Oh! for God's sake, my dear fellow—don't!" I entreated, as though he had hurt me. "All right. I'll shut up now and henceforth. Can't prevent me thinking though. . . . Never mind! . . . I'll show yet . . ." He went to the door in a hurry, paused with his head down, and came back, stepping deliberately. "I always thought that if a fellow could begin with a clean slate . . . And now you . . . in a measure . . . yes . . . clean slate." I waved my hand, and he marched out without looking back; the sound of his footfalls died out gradually behind the closed door—the unhesitating tread of a man walking in broad daylight.
>
> But as to me, left alone with the solitary candle, I remained strangely unenlightened. (185)

So indirect, difficult, and fragmented is the novel—so filled is it with ellipses, simple and grand—that it qualifies its statements of faith indirectly, via its own near-uninterpretability, almost as soon as it makes them.

But *Lord Jim,* in the last analysis, does not completely undercut itself. The narration may admit to being a stammering, but it is a stammering that implies there is a full and coherent statement behind it, even if that fullness and coherency cannot be fully articulated. As Marlow puts it, "the last word is not said,—probably shall never be said. Are not our lives too short for that full utterance which through all our stammering is of course our only and abiding intention?" (225). The novel shows us how even inarticulateness may turn out to be a form of articulation, how a life may turn out to be larger and more complete than its utterance. When Jim tries, again and again, to stammer out to Marlow his gratitude for Marlow's putting him in touch with Stein, Marlow says, "I cut him short. He was not articulate. . . . I told him that if he owed this chance to any one especially, it was to an old Scot of whom he had never heard, who had died many years ago, of whom little was remembered besides a roaring voice and a rough sort of honesty" (230).

Finally, the novel shows us, apparent senselessness may yield sense; there is, therefore, nobility in reaching for truth, even if often we seem to fail in our efforts, for often we succeed in the very moments in which we seem to fail. If we believe that, in the end, we have rescued some truth from the obscurity of the text—and that Marlow has rescued some truth from the obscurity of Jim's story—then we may well believe that Jim, too, has succeeded in the moment that he may seem to have failed: that he has reaffirmed the dream even as he has gained terrible self-knowledge. Jim is, after all, much like Marlow, who succeeds in spite of (perhaps because of) his stammering failure to state truth directly. And Jim, too, is "one of us"; he is, therefore, like all of us who as readers have achieved—however we explain it—the end of our quest for meaning by reaching the novel's last, baffling words: "Who knows? He is gone, inscrutable at heart, and the poor girl is leading a sort of soundless, inert life in Stein's house. Stein has aged greatly of late. He feels it himself, and says often he is 'preparing to leave all this; preparing to leave . . .' while he waves his hand sadly at his butterflies" (417).

Notes and References

1. Biographical Background

1. Leo Gurko, *Joseph Conrad: Giant in Exile* (New York: Macmillan, 1962), 16; hereafter cited in text.

2. *A Personal Record* (New York: Doubleday, Page, 1924), 120–21.

3. Norman Sherry, *Conrad's Eastern World* (Cambridge, England: Cambridge University Press, 1966), 7; hereafter cited in text.

4. *Straits Times Overland Journal,* October 22, 1881.

5. John Batchelor, *Lord Jim* (London: Urwin Hyman, 1988), 73; hereafter cited in text.

3. Critical Reception

1. Norman Sherry, ed., *Conrad: The Critical Heritage* (London: Routledge, 1973), 125–26; hereafter cited in text.

2. Gustav Morf, *The Polish Heritage of Joseph Conrad* (London: Sampson, Low, Marston, 1930), 149; hereafter cited in text.

3. Bernard C. Meyer, *Joseph Conrad: A Psychoanalytic Biography* (Princeton, N.J.: Princeton University Press, 1967), 63–64.

4. F. R. Leavis, *The Great Tradition* (1948; reprint, London: Peregrine, 1962), 177; hereafter cited in text.

5. Dorothy Van Ghent, *The English Novel: Form and Function* (New York: Rinehart, 1953), 235; hereafter cited in text.

6. Thomas Moser, *Joseph Conrad: Achievement and Decline,* (Cambridge, Mass.: Harvard University Press, 1957), 15–16; hereafter cited in text.

7. Albert J. Guerard, *Conrad the Novelist* (Cambridge, Mass.: Harvard University Press, 1958), 82, 84; hereafter cited in text.

8. Royal Roussel, *The Metaphysics of Darkness,* (Baltimore, Md.: Johns Hopkins University Press, 1971), vii–viii; hereafter cited in text.

9. Bruce Johnson, *Conrad's Models of Mind,* (Minneapolis: University of Minnesota Press, 1971), 65; hereafter cited in text.

10. David Thorburn, *Conrad's Romanticism,* (New Haven, Conn.: Yale University Press, 1974), 42; hereafter cited in text.

11. Ian Watt, *Conrad in the Nineteenth Century* (London: Chatto and Windus, 1979) 173; hereafter cited in text.

12. Daniel R. Schwarz, *Conrad: "Almayer's Folly" to "Under Western Eyes"* (London: Macmillan, 1980), 82; hereafter cited in text.

13. Fredric Jameson, *The Political Unconscious: Narrative as a Socially Symbolic Act* (London: Methuen, 1981), 628.

14. Suresh Raval, *The Art of Failure: Conrad's Fiction* (London: Allen and Unwin, 1986), 68; hereafter cited in text.

Selected Bibliography

Primary Works

The Text

The authoritative text of *Lord Jim* is the one found in the collected edition of the writer's works published by Heinemann in London and, in New York, by Doubleday and Company (1920). The novel was reprinted without change in subsequent Doubleday editions and, after that, in various Modern Library editions of the novel published by Random House. This study of the novel refers to page numbers in all the aforementioned, nearly identical Doubleday editions. The Signet (New American Library) edition also follows the 1920 Doubleday text, but its pagination is somewhat different.

Conrad's Letters

Karl, Frederick R., and Laurence Davies. *The Collected Letters of Joseph Conrad* (Cambridge, England: Cambridge University Press, 1983–88). The standard edition of Conrad's letters, it contains material previously published in other sources and collections, plus new letters, never before published. Volume 1 (covering 1861–97) was published in 1983, volume 2 (1898–1902) in 1986, and volume 3 (1903–07) in 1988. Until this edition has been published in its entirety, the best single source of letters written after 1907 will remain G. Jean-Aubry's *Joseph Conrad: Life and Letters* (London: Heinemann, 1927).

Secondary Works

Biographies

Jean-Aubry, G. *The Sea-Dreamer: A Definitive Biography of Joseph Conrad.* London: Allen and Unwin, 1957. Despite the title, and Jean-Aubry's claim, in the foreword, to have "set down the indisputable facts" in "the precise and detached fashion of a ship's log," this early biography—written in French and translated into English by Helen Sebba—is now thought to be factually unreliable in places. Jean-Aubry uses Conrad's fiction to advance his central thesis, namely, that Conrad's art faithfully represents scenes and moments from his life.

Karl, Frederick R. *Joseph Conrad: The Three Lives.* New York: Farrar, Straus, and Giroux, 1979. Almost 1,000 pages long and containing dozens of fascinating photographs and illustrations, Karl's is the standard biography of Conrad. As editor of the letters (many never before published), Karl was able to bring new information to light, especially about the second half of the writer's life. Karl's title refers to Conrad's life first as a Pole, later as a sailor, and finally as a writer. A Freudian, Karl often uses psychoanalytic theory to speculate not only about Conrad's life but also about his art.

Najder, Zdzislaw. *Joseph Conrad: A Chronicle.* New Brunswick, N.J.: Rutgers University Press, 1983. Published in the same year in England by Cambridge University Press, the Najder biography, now in its second printing in America, is the work of the foremost Polish Conrad scholar. Focusing on Conrad's personality and its relationship to the author's writings, the Najder biography, well translated by Halina Carroll-Najder and already in its second printing in the United States, makes for a useful and fascinating complement to the Karl biography, particularly since it is written by one who shares with Conrad a Polish heritage.

Watt, Ian. *Conrad in the Nineteenth Century.* Berkeley: University of California Press, 1979. Covering Conrad's early career (up to and just through *Lord Jim*), this fine study is a somewhat unusual biography, even though each of its five chapters begins with interesting, sometimes new biographical material. The emphasis of the book is on Conrad's relationship, as a writer, to nineteenth-century intellectual and aesthetic movements—such as romanticism, impressionism, and symbolism.

Critical Studies

Note: the following is a selected list of books on Conrad that contain significant discussions of *Lord Jim.*

Selected Bibliography

Batchelor, John. *Lord Jim.* London: Unwin Hyman, 1988. A book entirely devoted to *Lord Jim,* Batchelor's study contains chapters on "The Biographical Background," "The Critical Reception and Literary Context," and "Composition and Sources." An interesting comparison of Shakespeare's *Hamlet,* Calderon's *La Vida es Sueno,* and *Lord Jim* follows a long, chapter-by-chapter reading of Conrad's novel.

Gurko, Leo. *Joseph Conrad: Giant in Exile.* New York: Macmillan, 1962. A critical study of Conrad's major works that tends to sum up plot interpretively. Gurko bases his reading of *Lord Jim* on the French lieutenant's statement that "man is born a coward" but behaves well "out of necessity," owing to the "eye of others."

Johnson, Bruce. *Conrad's Models of Mind.* Minneapolis: University of Minnesota Press, 1971. A literary critic deeply influenced by philosophical thought—especially that of Schopenhauer and the existentialists—Johnson is interested in what he calls the "psychology of self-image." He focuses on the way in which Conrad's characters struggle to create their own identity and world in the face of an unexpectedly hostile and alienating one. Chapters are devoted to the following major works—*Almayer's Folly, The Nigger of the Narcissus,* "Heart of Darkness," *Lord Jim, Nostromo,* and *Victory*—plus other, lesser-known novels and tales.

Kuehn, Robert E., ed. *Twentieth-Century Interpretations of "Lord Jim."* Englewood Cliffs, N.J.: Prentice Hall, 1969. This volume contains reprints of some of the classic, older studies of the novel, including several that are summed up in chapter 3 of this study (those by Guerard and Van Ghent) and several excellent ones that are not. Of the latter, see especially "*Lord Jim:* From Sketch to Novel," by Eloise Knapp Hay; "Guilt and Atonement in *Lord Jim,*" by Jocelyn Baines; "*Lord Jim* and the Loss of Eden," by Paul Wiley; and "Butterflies and Beetles—Conrad's Two Truths," by Tony Tanner.

Meyer, Bernard C. *Joseph Conrad: A Psychoanalytic Biography.* Princeton, N.J.: Princeton University Press, 1967. This study, written by an M.D., psychoanalyzes Conrad through his texts and also sees Conrad's works as being about the influence of unconscious forces on behavior. Meyer agrees with Morf (see later entry) that the *Patna* represents Poland, and he goes even further, suggesting that Jim's desertion of his ship represents Conrad's subconscious feeling that he was somehow partly responsible for his mother's death.

Morf, Gustav. *The Polish Heritage of Joseph Conrad.* London: Sampson, Low, Marston, 1930. This classic critical biography, which has greatly influenced Conrad criticism, was republished by Haskell House in 1965. After devoting four chapters to "The Ancestors," "The Parents," "The Boy," and "The Man," Morf turns to Conrad's fiction (particularly to *Lord Jim,* and *Nostromo*). He argues that *Lord Jim* expresses, in thinly disguised terms, the lifelong guilt Conrad felt over his abandonment of

Poland. Appendixes include an essay by the psychoanalytic theorist Carl Gustav Jung on the "introvert intuitive type" of personality, plus essays written and published in Polish newspapers and journals.

Moser, Thomas. *Joseph Conrad: Achievement and Decline*. Cambridge, Mass.: Harvard University Press, 1957. A general psychological study, not so much of Conrad as of his characters, which Moser divides into three major types: the "simple hero," the "vulnerable hero," and the "perceptive hero." This brief study spans Conrad's entire career in four chapters and, to a greater or lesser extent, covers all of the author's well-known works.

Page, Norman. *A Conrad Companion*. New York: St. Martin's Press, 1986. An extremely handy reference, this volume includes an extensive "Conrad Chronology" followed by "A Conrad Who's Who"; an introduction to "Conrad's World" (complete with a number of instructive maps); chapters on the novels and stories that provide information on contexts, composition, and publication history; and an appendix devoted to film versions of Conrad's works.

Raval, Suresh. *The Art of Failure: Conrad's Fiction*. Boston: Allen and Unwin, 1986. A study of Conrad's major works, this book includes chapters on "Heart of Darkness," *Lord Jim, Nostromo, The Secret Agent, Under Western Eyes,* and *Victory*. Raval's thesis is that Conrad and his characters are involved in a difficult, often-doomed struggle to understand—and to communicate their understanding of—a complex, perhaps-ultimately-baffling reality. At the heart of Conrad's fiction, according to Raval, is an almost paradoxical skepticism about the possibility of knowing and communicating through language, including literary language.

Roussel, Royal. *The Metaphysics of Darkness: A Study of the Unity and Development of Conrad's Fiction*. Baltimore, Md.: Johns Hopkins University Press, 1971. A phenomenological approach to Conrad, this study attempts to discover the unity or coherence of the author's lifework, or oeuvre, the fundamental vision or understanding that was central to Conrad's consciousness and played out in everything he ever wrote. Ignoring chronological order and discussing early and late works together, Roussel finds in all of them a concern with reassuring but misleading surfaces or appearances—like the peaceful surface of the sea described in *Lord Jim* just before the *Patna* strikes a floating derelict.

Schwarz, Daniel R. *Conrad: "Almayer's Folly" to "Under Western Eyes."* Ithaca, N.Y.: Cornell University Press, 1980. A study of roughly the first half of Conrad's career as a writer, Schwarz's book is divided into two parts. Part 1, "Quest for Identity," includes a chapter entitled "The Journey to Patusan: The Education of Jim and Marlow in *Lord Jim*"; part 2, "Politics," focuses on *Nostromo, The Secret Agent,* and *Under Western*

Eyes. Schwarz differs from (a majority of) critics, from F. R. Leavis to Fredric Jameson, in arguing that the Patusan episode is not disappointing and anticlimactic but, rather, necessary and even instrumental to the development of the novel's two main characters and central meanings.

Sherry, Norman. *Conrad's Eastern World.* Cambridge, England: Cambridge University Press, 1966. As chapter 1 of this volume suggests, Sherry's study offers the most exhaustive (and also the most interesting) account of the parallels between Conrad's experiences as a sailor and the stories he tells in major works set in the East. In addition to providing backgrounds to *Lord Jim*, Sherry provides contexts for *Almayer's Folly, An Outcast of the Islands, The End of the Tether*, and *The Shadow Line*.

———, ed. *Conrad: The Critical Heritage.* London: Routledge and Kegan Paul, 1973. An anthology of early reviews of all the novels and volumes of stories published by Conrad over a 30-year period, from *Almayer's Folly* (1895) to *Suspense* (1925). The editor's introduction to the volume provides a brief overview of what is to follow—plus some comments by Conrad on his own work and its critical reception.

Thorburn, David. *Conrad's Romanticism.* New Haven, Conn.: Yale University Press, 1974. As its title implies, this study demonstrates those ways in which Conrad's literary art builds on and develops that of the English romantics. Thorburn, who considers several varieties of romanticism (not only that of the English romantic poets but also that of the adventure tale in the style of Robert Louis Stevenson), argues that Conrad is particularly influenced by romantic modes of storytelling (Marlow, in "Heart of Darkness," is compared with Coleridge's Ancient Mariner). Thorburn's intent is not to deny Conrad a place in the modern tradition but, rather, to argue, following Robert Langbaum, for the romantic roots of modernism.

INDEX

Index

The Author

Ross C Murfin is a professor of English and dean of the College of Arts and Sciences at the University of Miami. His previously published works include *Swinburne, Hardy, Lawrence and the Burden of Belief, The Poetry of D. H. Lawrence: Texts and Contexts,* and *"Sons and Lovers": A Novel of Division and Desire.* He has edited two volumes devoted to Conrad: *Conrad Revisited: Essays for the 80's* and *"Heart of Darkness": A Case Study in Contemporary Criticism.*